"Getting young people started in the right direction creates a gift that will serve them their entire lives. *The EduNinja Mindset* inspires and provides actionable ways to be a Ninja in and out of the classroom. We need as many hands on deck to support each other and young humans finding their way. Life is full of obstacles, but when you have a plan and a clear path it makes getting through them so much easier. Jen knows this firsthand, and I am so grateful to her for sharing her message with all of us. It does take a village, but why not a village of Ninjas?"

—Gabrielle Reece, health and fitness expert, model, and author

"We knew Jen Burdis would be an inspirational force addressing our faculty, and she didn't disappoint. The combined skill sets of an elite athlete and a master teacher incarnate in one person! Jen's story is one of success through resiliency, integrity, and fortitude. Educators everywhere can draw inspiration from her example."

—Dr. John Skretta, superintendent of Norris School District

"An incredible, inspirational book about reaching for personal greatness inside and outside the classroom."

—Jon Gordon, author of *The Energy Bus* and *The Carpenter*

"*The EduNinja Mindset* epitomizes the journey of Jen, a small-town girl with a learning disability, to a big-time role model with a plan to help others. She never gave less than her best and did it with a smile."

—Russ Rose, Penn State women's volleyball coach

"Jen is a true inspiration to me. I remember how hard she worked when we were in college. She was always looking for ways to be her best and, even more importantly, ways to help others be their best. When I saw that she was competing as a Ninja Warrior and teaching, I was inspired again. I am so happy so many more people will be able to hear her story and be inspired through this book."

—**Kerry McCoy,** head wrestling coach, University of Maryland,
former head wrestling coach at Stanford University,
2x US Olympian, world championship silver medalist,
2x NCAA national champion, 3x NCAA All American

"Jennifer Burdis is one of the most inspirational, genuine people I've ever met. Jen is truly a guiding light for anyone looking to live a healthier lifestyle. *The EduNinja Mindset* is a must-read for anyone hoping to live their best life."

—**Adam Taliaferro,** New Jersey state legislator,
former Penn State football letterman, motivational speaker

"Be prepared to take a journey towards wellness, awareness, and fun with Jennifer Burdis. She has written a book that will both enhance and challenge. *The EduNinja Mindset* will invite balance into your life in a way that is transformative. Imagine reading this book and having a sincere, supportive force like Jennifer Burdis encouraging you to reach new heights—making you a better person for yourself and others. *The EduNinja Mindset* is not just about fitness and exercise; it is an intentional approach for educators to revolutionize their lives by being better for others. You are taking a bold, giant step in reading this book, and Jen Burdis' inspiring and motivating words will change your life."

—**Sean Gaillard,** principal, Lexington Middle School,
author of *The Pepper Effect*

"Jen's 'journey' is nothing short of amazing! As one of her former high school teachers and coaches, Jen's road to fulfillment is not surprising. *The EduNinja Mindset* is who Jen is, and her inspiration, passion, and commitment makes her the perfect role model for students and educators alike. I am moved by her mind/body insight, reflection, and her path to living a full and healthy life."

—Peg Pennepacker, CAA, high school Title IX consulting services

Jennifer Burdis

The EduNinja Mindset

11 **Habits for Building a Stronger**
Mind and **Body**

The EduNinja Mindset

© 2018 by Jennifer Burdis

This book is available at special discounts when purchased in quantity for use as premiums, promotions, fundraisers, or for educational use. For inquiries and details, contact the publisher at books@daveburgessconsulting.com.

Published by Dave Burgess Consulting, Inc.
San Diego, CA
DaveBurgessConsulting.com

Cover Design by Genesis Kohler
Editing and Interior Design by My Writers' Connection

Library of Congress Control Number: 2018942306
Paperback ISBN: 978-1-946444-83-7
Ebook ISBN: 978-1-946444-84-4

First Printing: May 2018

Dedication

This book is dedicated in loving memory to Penn State Volleyball teammate and friend, Samantha Spink Ramsay, who will forever be remembered for her spunk and zeal for life.

Contents

Introduction

As an elementary teacher with almost two decades of experience, I've embraced the role of helping students of all ages reach for their personal greatness, both in and out of the classroom. I've learned that when people incorporate positive, sustained strategies to increase daily activity, mindfulness, and thoughtful food choices, they achieve more.

While earning an elementary education degree and a minor in kinesiology as a Penn State student athlete, I was fortunate to work with trainers, a sports psychologist, and a sports nutritionist to help build a priceless foundation of healthy habits. These experts all stressed the importance of daily physical activity, mind-body connection, and making healthy food choices to create a happy and successful life.

After my dad's triple bypass heart surgery seven years ago, I wanted to show him—and others—that it can be easy to lead a healthier life. Competing in seasons six and seven of NBC's *American Ninja Warrior* as the "EduNinja" reinforced my commitment to empowering my parents, coworkers, students, and their families to pursue healthier goals.

As a NSCA-Certified Personal Trainer, the more I learned about nutrition, movement, and mindfulness, the more I wanted to share that information with teachers so they could use it themselves and share these health strategies with their students and families. Teaching is empowering yet exhausting. We find ourselves working overtime—staying up late to grade papers or give feedback on essays, coming into work early to set up our amazing science experiment, and working through lunch so we can go home early. It's this vicious pattern that, if sustained for long periods, can lead to chronic fatigue and, eventually, burnout. That's why we need tools to help us catch the warning signs early and start making positive, healthy changes.

Our students also need these tools to help them be ready and effective learners. Our job is to help students find their strengths, develop their unique skills, and empower them with tools to help them on their learning paths—paths often filled with big and frightening obstacles. To do our job well, we must first recognize our own obstacles as beautiful challenges meant to reveal our very best and become teachers who raise the bar to strive for personal greatness. In doing so, we inspire our students to do the same.

Speaking of beautiful obstacles, my first concern when thinking about sharing what I had learned was, *How can I share this message? Writing a book would be impossible; I'm dyslexic!* Honestly, I had fourth graders in my class who were better writers than I was. But my desire to share this information and help others surpassed any fleeting thought of quitting because of my dyslexic struggles. Besides, I knew quite a bit about overcoming obstacles I thought I had no business even attempting—and I knew that beating the odds felt amazing and that doing so made my life better. I knew that writing this book and sharing my message would help people overcome their own challenges and make their lives better.

So I pushed past my comfort zone to open up to my learning struggles, share tough times in my life, present lessons learned, and offer health and wellness strategies for teachers, families, and students. That is how *The EduNinja Mindset* was born.

What Is the EduNinja Mindset?

The EduNinja Mindset is all about striving to achieve personal greatness. It's about embracing challenges, knowing you'll come out stronger—regardless of whether you fail or succeed. It's committing to conquer a beastly new challenge—and recommitting when someone raises the bar a tad higher. With an EduNinja Mindset, setbacks don't discourage you; they fuel you to learn more, prepare smarter, and train harder. You know effort and failure are necessary to grow and master useful skills. It's the attitude that empowers you to respond to the question, *What am I going to do with this obstacle? Whatever it takes!* It's finding the courage to look your fears in the face, grapple with them, and conquer them. It's grinding past your challenges and finding a way (or *making* a way) to overcome them. It's working each and every day to grow physically, mentally, and spiritually. And it's empowering others to believe in themselves and achieve their own personal greatness.

The EduNinja Mindset advocates that it doesn't matter where you start, which prevents you from comparing your ability to someone else's. With this mindset, you focus on working to the best of your ability, knowing even your most basic skill in any area can be developed through dedication and hard work. It's what allows you to feel proud of working up to your potential. It's what pushes you to apply and practice willpower by holding your goal front and center, displaying hard work every day, and surrounding yourself with others who will support you as you fail, learn, and use corrective feedback to eventually get better despite your setbacks.

Join me as I share my story of what school was like for me, how I found the strength to keep overcoming obstacles, the mentors who gave me tools to eventually succeed, and how I apply this mindset—and its corresponding strategies and daily healthy habits—to empower my students to develop the life skills they need to conquer the obstacles in their path. By sharing my story with you, I hope to convince you that when you possess the right *mindset, grit,* and *passion,* you have power to accomplish your biggest goals and make a unique contribution to your community.

It's time to raise the bar for your life with *The EduNinja Mindset!*

An EduNinja
Overcomes Obstacles

Our greatest weakness lies in giving up.
The most certain way to succeed is
always to try just one more time.

—Thomas A. Edison

Tell me and I forget. Teach me and I
remember. Involve me and I learn.

—Benjamin Franklin

As I stood on the steps of one of the tallest and brightest obstacle courses in history, I felt amped, focused, and ready for the challenge ahead of me. In my periphery, I saw the cameras, crew, and bright lights illuminating the obstacles in my path. A surge of energy rushed through my body. I took a few slow, deep breaths and focused on the first obstacle, a set of five massive steps. My strategy was to leap across the "Jen-sized" gap and embrace each step with a giant hug to avoid falling into the cold water below.

Everything slowed and became silent, fading to the background. The din of the audience in the bleachers, directions being barked at the crew who moved about quickly to fulfill them, and the conversations of other athletes behind me faded until all I could see was the course before me. Staring straight ahead, I focused on taking one step at a time. Then the cue came from a crew member who looked at me and said, "This is your world; I'm just living in it." I knew at that moment I had trained relentlessly for this course—for the opportunity to become a Ninja Warrior. This was my chance.

Fully focused "in the zone," I did a few knee-tuck jumps and then exploded up and off the platform with all my effort toward the first step. The moment I leapt through the air, I realized the steps were farther apart than I anticipated. Each step would require every inch I could muster. My five-foot-two-inch frame landed on the first obstacle, and I white knuckled the sides to avoid falling into the cold water below. I glanced over my right shoulder, across the water behind me, to jump off the first step, flinging my body into the air again and grabbing onto the second mist-covered step as my feet flirted with slipping into the water. Each successful leap felt like a momentous accomplishment of effort and concentration. As I gratefully completed the fifth and final step of this first obstacle, I was already breathing as if I had just run an entire mile—and I still had five more obstacles to face. There was no time to rest since the next obstacle was waiting for me.

I greeted the second obstacle with a huge smile, happy to see a slackline ladder bridge made of what looked like two extremely long, loose "seat belts." I had some experience crossing slack lines; I'd used them in my training. I slowly shimmied my feet along the narrow bands as one would across the ocean floor to avoid stepping on a jellyfish. Maintaining this slow and steady strategy, time felt like it slowed as I literally focused on each foot slide across this bridge. Near the halfway point I started feeling my legs, which reminded me they were working to help get me across. I finally took my last few shuffles across the slackline and stepped onto the platform to face the next obstacle. My body trembled from the tremendous amount of exertion

I had already expended. My legs were pumped and so was I, feeling like I just finished "leg day" at the gym after successfully completing the second obstacle.

Next, I faced an obstacle that had thrown many experienced competitors into the cold water below. This upright, human-sized, spinning wheel perched high above the water. I pressed my body flush against it, barely shoving and squeezing my quadruple-knotted sneakers into the toe clips, while grabbing the mounted grips with my tiny hands. I nudged the wheel to see how much force it really had. Immediately, the wheel took off with my entire body attached by my will. It accelerated quickly downhill, trying to make me another one of its victims. The force pulling at me was something I'd only felt while getting thrown in Brazilian jiu-jitsu. With one completed forceful revolution, I continued to press my shoulder deeper into the side of the disc while it rolled upside down with me still in it. I pushed up and into my shoulders with maximum effort like a handstand push-up, then pressed forcefully down into my legs as the wheel completed a second revolution, not sure if I'd be able to hang on for the third. With dogged determination, I hung on. A bit dizzy and winded when I finally untensed and peeled my body from the disc, I couldn't help feeling elated to have escaped the wrath of the spinning wheel!

At the fourth obstacle, the lights seemed brighter and TV cameras closer as I stood in front of a mini trampoline, craning to look up at a bar that appeared to be a mile above me. My goal was to bounce on the trampoline to create enough lift so I could grab hold of the bar. I walked up to the trampoline and took a few testing bounces; I'd never jumped off a trampoline before. With a better idea of what to expect from the jump, I took a few steps back then raced forward and hit the trampoline hard with both feet. It worked—sort of. I flew up and touched the bar with my fingertips. Unfortunately, I didn't have quite enough height to grab the bar and hang on. Down I went, landing with a splash in the water pit below. My first *American Ninja Warrior* adventure was over, but I wasn't going to let that stop me from moving forward.

The biggest obstacles I've had to overcome in my life weren't the ones I faced on the *American Ninja Warrior* course. Nor were they ones I encountered during my hours of intense training. Instead, I faced my greatest obstacles as a student—trying to navigate my way through the pages of a book, spell simple words correctly, and avoid class discussions. In fact, I didn't learn to read until I was in my master's program—in *reading and writing curriculum instruction*. Yes, post-college. You see, I have dyslexia. And if you're thinking this doesn't make sense, especially for an educator at a high performing school, you're right. But it is true. Dyslexia made my learning path extremely challenging, but it also afforded me the unique opportunity

"… dyslexic/ADHD kids are creative, "outside-the-box" thinkers. They have to be, because they don't see or solve problems the same way other kids do. In school, unfortunately, they are sometimes written off as lazy, unmotivated, rude, or even stupid. They aren't. If they can get through their rough school years, they often go on to become very successful adults. Employers love them, because they come up with original, fresh ideas. Making Percy ADHD/dyslexic was my way of honoring the potential of all the kids I've known who have those conditions. It's not a bad thing to be different. Sometimes, it's the mark of being very, very talented."

—**Rick Riordan**, author of the *Percy Jackson* series

to embrace grit and develop expansive creative problem-solving skills to overcome obstacles in my life—which ultimately developed into my EduNinja Mindset.

Never Underestimate the Underdog

In March of 2015, I was just a few days away from running the *American Ninja Warrior* course for the second year in a row. After my rookie season, I knew what to expect and made focused training—of my body *and* my mind—a priority. I spent the entire year preparing for the competition. To mentally prepare, I read Malcolm Gladwell's *David and Goliath: Underdogs, Misfits, and the Art of Battling Giants.* It seemed to be a perfect fit; I am a fan of underdogs.

Growing up in Orwigsburg, Pennsylvania—a small, remote, rural farming town, tucked into the southern end of a coal mining county near the Appalachian Mountains—provided a lot of opportunities for me to root for the underdogs. I grew up identifying with the underdogs of books, movies, and life who worked so hard to win, and I looked up to them. One of these underdogs—Muhammad Ali—built his training camp a few miles from my parents' house. You may not remember Ali as an underdog, but when he faced (and defeated) the almost unbeatable World Heavyweight Champion Sonny Liston for the world heavyweight championship on February 25, 1964, he *was* an underdog.

My grandma and dad were underdogs also. Both grew up in Minersville, Pennsylvania, and embodied the coal mining mentality of working hard to accomplish goals, persevering, and being grateful no matter what the circumstances. I always looked up to my grandma. Out of my four grandparents, she was the only one to go to high school. My grandpa completed eighth grade, while my other grandma and my grandpa completed sixth and eighth grade respectively. My grandma was a special winner to me. Dad was another underdog winner. My dad woke up at 5 a.m. to complete his early-morning paper route before school. The title of the newspaper was fittingly titled *Grit*. After graduating from a high school where there were fifty boys in every class (can you imagine the rowdy learning environment created by having *fifty* boys in your class), he went on to be the first in his family to graduate from college. Throughout much of my childhood, he commuted an hour and a half each way to work every day—a sacrifice for which I will always be grateful. In addition to being an electrical engineer, my dad served on the town's borough council for seven years, was president for four years, and even our Little League baseball coach. My grandma and dad both told stories of the importance of hard work and not worrying about what others think. Their example helped me understand that being the first to do something—even something others say is crazy or impossible—should be celebrated. So the fact I was about to take a second run at the *American Ninja Warrior* course as an underdog—a five-foot-two-inch, thirty-nine-year-old female—seemed fitting.

You Wouldn't Wish Dyslexia on Your Child, or Would You?

A few nights before the competition, I got to Chapter 4, David Boies' contribution to *David and Goliath*: "You Wouldn't Wish Dyslexia on Your Child, or Would You?" where I read, "Dyslexia is a problem in the way people hear and manipulate sounds. The difference between bah and dah is a subtlety in the first forty milliseconds of the syllable."

Wow! What a coincidence this was mentioned. My family called my grandma "Bah." As a child, I could never pronounce "Grandma." I always said "Bah" instead.

The next day, my parents arrived from Pennsylvania to watch my *American Ninja Warrior* run, and my mom handed me an old childhood *Fraggle Rock* book she recently found. When I opened the book, I found a bookmark I had made for my grandma. It said, "My Book Marqir. Fo Bha, Form Jennifer." I had crossed out and changed "Marqir" to "Marker" and "Form" to "From," but I had never changed the rest. I looked at the bookmark, remembering carefully picking those three different colors of paper and skillfully ripping the two kinds of tape to carefully wrap around the paper. I looked at the bookmark and the book and then told my mom I had never read the book because it had too many words.

As I continued reading *David and Goliath*, I felt like I was reading symptoms on Web MD perfectly matching my own. On page 102 of the book, Nadine Gaab, a dyslexia researcher at Harvard, said:

> *If you have no concept of sound or language, it might take you a while to read, then you may read so slowly you lose comprehension, and then can't read content in middle school. Usually you get a diagnosis at eight or nine (or thirty-nine) and we find by that point there are already a lot of serious psychological implications, because by that time you've been struggling for three years . . . . Your peers may think you're stupid. Your parents may think you're lazy. You have very low self-esteem, which leads to an increased rate of depression. Kids with dyslexia are more likely to end up in the juvenile system, because they act up. It's because they can't figure things out. It's so important in our society to read.*

★ 7 ★

The bookmark, *Fraggle Rock* book, and Gaab's words made me think back to the small private grade school I attended. Although I have no other memories of first or second grade, I do remember that my teacher placed me in the green "middle" reading group. Of course, we were supposed to know how to read by third grade, but by then, I had missed my reading window of opportunity. Instead, I did a lot of non-reading, short story cards, guessing the answers, and independently checking my measly odds of getting them correct.

On the long, uphill walk home, my backpack was always heavy, filled with workbooks and worksheets I couldn't do in class because I couldn't read the directions. I could only guess at the answers. Clearly, those workbook pages didn't help me learn. In middle school, I would ask other students about the directions on worksheets and then guess my way through questions. Learning to manage worksheets by asking and guessing would become my saving grace for schoolwork.

I never heard what other students read out loud in class because I spent the whole time trying to guess what I'd be reading before it was my turn. As a result, I missed the majority of content. In this downward spiral, I never spoke up in class conversations because I didn't know the content or the answers, and I fervently hoped I wouldn't get called on to answer any questions.

I didn't just struggle in reading class; I struggled in *all* my classes. I got low scores on my multiplication quizzes in math and rarely spelled anything correctly in any class unless I could find it printed somewhere. Still today I have to purposefully think about my address, zip code, and other numbers to be sure I don't mix them up. And I have a difficult time typing my password the same way twice. Even Twitter chats create anxiety because it's challenging for me to read responses and answer in a timely manner without making mistakes.

I probably learned the most in my middle school science class because we weren't required to read to get the information. My teacher was Mr. Kulich, a diehard Boston Celtics fan who also coached me in volleyball and basketball. Telling sports stories of Larry Bird and college athletes related to the science lessons, he knew what motivated his students. We were hooked, always totally engaged in his lessons, eager to hear what he said next. Mr. Kulich used experiments, videos, and hands-on projects, and offered so many concept-to-life connections. As a result, I finally experienced lessons I could remember. He was meeting my unique learning needs.

Prior to Mr. Kulich's classes, I had developed ways to "succeed in the system," but I didn't feel like a successful student. Instead of feeling confident, motivated, and engaged in the lessons, I felt anxious, lost, and alone. But because I could understand the way he taught— and his passion for science and sports—I learned the most from him.

Sports became my other teacher. The basketball court, volleyball court, and the Little League baseball field were my learning venues. There, my hard work paid off, and in 1988, I was fortunate to be the first girl in our town's history to make the Little League All-Star team, despite many people thinking girls shouldn't be playing. My experiences on the athletic field offered valuable life lessons; they are where I developed a mindset to persevere and problem-solve. However, it took a couple more years for that mindset to follow me to school.

Transitioning from a small first through eighth grade school where I "passed with honors," somehow getting 80 percent and above in my subjects, to a big public high school felt intimidating, challenging, and demoralizing. I succeeded in sports but struggled in the classroom trying to navigate a slew of obstacles. I just didn't have the tools. Attempting to pass my freshmen classes—with triple the workload and without any real academic skills—was next to impossible.

In addition to the actual work, there were also social ramifications. Could you imagine being a high schooler having never read a single book? Just trying to understand the directions was a challenge, let alone being able to read a textbook for content, synthesize information, and then share what I learned by answering questions out loud. Forget about it. I couldn't even fully read CliffsNotes for novels because it was too much reading for me. I found myself always asking friends what I missed in every single class because I didn't (and couldn't) do the reading. As a result, I may have appeared lazy or stupid to my peers, and possibly my teachers, but in fact I just couldn't read. I was getting many Cs, Ds, and Fs.

But there was still another layer to my situation. To hide the fact that I couldn't read, my strategy was to be quiet in class—always. I wanted to be invisible so no one would call on me or ask me what I learned. This learned behavior served as camouflage, allowing me to blend into the background without being seen. This way I didn't draw attention to myself. As a result, I learned my voice wasn't important and didn't need to be heard because I would most likely be wrong if I tried to answer a question.

So on top of a reading deficiency, low grades, and an uncomfortable social situation, I then had a hard time communicating with people. I always practiced being quiet the majority of my day instead of developing communication skills. This negatively affected my own self-esteem and self-talk. I didn't have anyone to boost me up, and I also lacked the internal strength or tools to boost myself up.

I felt stupid, alone, and like an outsider, but I didn't fully know why. Almost every interaction I had—in a class, with a teacher, or with another student—proved I had no idea what was going on. School did not empower or inspire me. Instead, it reinforced my belief that I was a failure.

During my sophomore year, I flunked geometry and was on my way to failing Spanish. After another failed test, my Spanish teacher, Señora Froling, told me she didn't think my problem was a lack of knowledge of the material. She pointed to one of the many red marks on my page, one next to the word "Flordia," and asked, "What do you notice about this?" I had no idea what she was referring to. She said "Flordia" is really spelled F-l-o-r-i-d-a. *Oh whatever*, I told myself again. I just mixed up the letters. However, she revealed the root of these spelling errors could likely be dyslexia.

Mrs. Froling was the first person (and remains the only person) who ever told me I might have dyslexia. Interestingly, she taught Spanish—*not* English! Why would she suspect dyslexia when no one else had? For a split second, I thought maybe she was right. Every morning I drank orange juice from a plastic cup with "Florida" printed on it. Surely I should have known how to spell "Florida" since I saw it every day. But I didn't. (And to this day, I still have to think hard every time I spell it.) I didn't know what to do with her dyslexia hypothesis, so I quickly dismissed it and assumed my Spanish teacher was wrong, though looking back now, she nailed it. I never shared this information with anyone. She never brought it up again, and no testing was ever done. I just pushed through, failing some classes and barely getting by in others.

By the end of my sophomore year, I felt helplessly behind and had no idea how to do any of my schoolwork. I *wanted* to do the work, but I didn't have the tools to begin to understand the questions. I'd try, but I felt I was wasting time and learning nothing. Dealing with the pressures of school and not being able to learn was bad enough, but I also had to cope with the anxiety of trying to make the required grades to stay on the sports teams. My only successes in high school came through volleyball, basketball, and competing in track and field. It was where I felt comfortable asking questions. I put in the effort and, for the first time in a school endeavor, saw positive results. My height was a disadvantage, but with practice, I mastered specific skills, like launching a javelin to qualify for state meets, defending talented opponents on the basketball court, and hitting crafty shots against taller blockers in volleyball. Most importantly, accomplishing these skills successfully with my teammates helped me feel good about myself. I received support from my coaches, family, friends, and teachers who came to cheer on our team as we competed. And through the experience, I learned numerous life lessons—from training, teamwork, and competing to be my personal best.

Do You Want to Play at Penn State?

The summer after my junior year, while attending Penn State's volleyball camp, I had a life-changing opportunity. I met Penn State's legendary women's volleyball coach, Russ Rose. Today, after the 2017 season, Coach Rose's resume spans thirty-nine years of coaching at Penn State and shines with 1,246 wins and only 198 losses, sixteen Big Ten Championships, and seven NCAA National Championship titles. He has helped produce multiple Olympians, 174 Academic All-Big-Ten selections, and twelve Academic All-Americans while maintaining elite expectations of himself, his athletes, and the Nittany Lion program.

To meet Coach Rose the summer before my high school senior year was an honor, in part because I didn't have the type of club volleyball experience that most players had. After the camp's preliminary athletic testing was done, I took my assigned spot on "court two" as a setter. It was an honor because five-foot-two-inch setters are almost unheard of in competitive volleyball. Early into the camp, my court coach told me Coach Rose wanted to talk to me. A rush of emotions flooded me. I was excited, intimidated, nervous, and scared. I slowly walked up to his office wondering what exactly this meeting was about. I sat down as he introduced himself and asked me a little bit about my volleyball background, my family, and where I grew up. Thankfully, in Russ Rose fashion, he didn't keep me waiting or guessing what this meeting was about; almost immediately he asked, "Do you want to play volleyball at Penn State?"

Did I want to play for Penn State? I was confused. Was he asking me a hypothetical question? My dad graduated from Penn State after returning from serving in the Navy. Growing up, we scheduled our Saturdays around Penn State football games and made a few trips up to State College to see the football and volleyball teams play. We even ate dinner under a huge Nittany Lion light hanging above our kitchen table! Of course I wanted to play for Penn State! But I'd only dreamed of it. I didn't really think Coach Rose was asking me to play for him. But after talking with him a bit more, I realized that's *exactly* what he was asking.

I couldn't believe it! He was giving me—a five-foot-two-inch "court two" volleyball camper—the opportunity to be a "walk on" player at Penn State! I had learned to play volleyball in middle school on a blacktop volleyball net strung between two tire-based poles

I couldn't believe it! He was giving me—a five-foot-two-inch "court two" volleyball camper—the opportunity to be a "walk on" player at Penn State!

since our school didn't have a gym until my eighth-grade year. I'd spent hours at home hitting and passing a volleyball off my rooftop in both middle and high school instead of playing on a big club volleyball team. What an opportunity! I couldn't wait to tell my family and friends.

As I started my senior year, I was excited for this new athletic opportunity that gave me hope and focus. However, this positivity just didn't translate into the classroom, where I unfortunately spent most of my day failing in much of my schoolwork. I successfully created every art project and dissected all the animal parts my anatomy teacher picked up from the local butcher. As a kinesthetic learner, those hands-on activities were the most memorable for me; however, these alone didn't earn me a high school diploma. In June, I was allowed to walk in our high school graduation ceremony, but I only received a blank piece of paper. I was headed to summer school to take English so I could actually graduate. Thankfully, the summer English class consisted only of grammar worksheets, so those workbook skills I learned in elementary school finally paid off. I passed with a 96 percent!

What Did I Get Myself Into?

At Penn State's freshman orientation during the summer, I walked into a huge auditorium, slumped into my chair, and opened a folder I'd been given. While I didn't realize it at the time, the data showed many things. I vaguely remembered seeing what I believed were my predicted odds of graduating: I believe it was less than 1 percent. I wish I still had that paper today to know if I even interpreted the data correctly, but I'll never forget that sinking feeling in my stomach. I was in trouble. *What did I get myself into?*

During our first one-on-one volleyball meeting, Coach Rose told me he expected me to win every suicide running drill in practice *and* achieve Academic All-Big Ten honors every year. I could potentially see winning running drills because I was quick. But making Academic All-Big Ten every year? This made no sense. I had struggled at school my entire life. I assumed Coach's expectations were the same for all the players, but when I asked my roommate if he had told her the same thing, she said, "No."

In August 1993, I arrived at Penn State and began the infamously grueling two weeks of preseason volleyball practice, ranging from six to nine hours a day. Each practice was mentally and physically challenging. Because I was a walk-on player, I had to work extra hard, competing for a spot on the team so I wouldn't be cut. Plus, because I'd been a small high school setter, Coach Rose decided to train me as a defensive specialist, which meant I was learning a position I knew absolutely nothing about. The original feelings of flattery I had when Coach asked me to walk on quickly disappeared as my lack of fundamental skills and club ball experience became apparent. Fortunately, my hard work on the court paid off. I made the team and was redshirted. This meant I was able to train with the team that first season to develop the defensive specialist skills and better learn collegiate volleyball, as long as I didn't play in any games that year. The good thing about redshirting is that it gives you a total of five years on the team, getting to play four seasons. This timeline also gave me the opportunity to earn a kinesiology minor and complete my student teaching.

In addition to the enormous challenges with volleyball, I also had to figure out how to be a college student at a notable academic school. I quickly learned that nothing about this college experience would be easy. But I was unwilling to let Coach Rose down, so I used every possible minute to plod through textbooks. For a nonreader, college is intimidating. I went to all of my classes, took notes, and even purchased "Nittany Notes," which are organized, logical notes taken by other students in the class which were then photocopied and sold to the public by a local business. But even these scaffolds took me forever to read; rereading them multiple times was necessary for me to try to learn information and memorize facts. I literally took these notes and used them to help me recreate new notes, highlighting and boxing words, and drawing words, symbols, and pictures. It was a repetitive ritual to help me learn, but it helped me access textbook information I hadn't been able to understand at first. Granted, I wasn't studying to be a rocket scientist, but for me, the general education classes required the same amount of effort others gave in far more difficult classes. Thankfully, all my note-reading and flash-card-making served me well enough to earn high test scores; Academic All-Big Ten Honors became a reality my first season.

During my freshman year, a weird shift started happening: I was succeeding academically, but volleyball was challenging. Ultimately, I'd spend three full years standing on the sidelines, cheering for my teammates—three years anxiously waiting to get Coach's nod for me to go in for a few plays—three years getting left behind when the team headed out to play in Hawaii or California or against other Big Ten conference teams because I didn't make the travel team. Three full years of training equated to *zero* playing time.

Despite my determined work ethic on the court, the disappointment of not getting any playing time for over three solid years wore on my soul. During my redshirt junior year, I decided I didn't want to be a part of the team anymore. I took the spring training season off while my teammates continued to train but, apparently, Coach Rose hadn't given up on me. My roommate kept coming back from training saying, "Coach is wondering if you'd come back to play?" The short break had given me time to refocus, and I was ready to start training again.

I'm grateful Coach Rose nudged me and gave me the opportunity to rejoin the team. And I'm thankful for the formula of sports, plus a mentor in a supportive environment, inspiring me to learn and grow over time. I'm thankful I didn't give up—on school or sports. I spent two more years on the Penn State volleyball team—earning Academic All-Big Ten Honors every single year, making new friends, and *playing* my last two seasons! I was part of three Big Ten Championships and played for Penn State's first national championship attempt, falling just short to Kerri Walsh's amazing Stanford team. Penn State has gone on to win seven national championships under Coach Rose. And while I was never a big hitter who got TV time or newspaper features, I worked hard day in and day out trying to be the best I could be. Today, I am extremely proud to be a part of the Penn State women's volleyball tradition.

From Obstacle to Strength

At first glance, dyslexia and being a five-foot-two-inch collegiate volleyball player were hardships. As a learner and an athlete, I had many frustrating obstacles to overcome. But I'm finally able to say dyslexia and my lack of height are both *strengths*—or at least provided opportunities for me to develop strengths. Through these obstacles, I have learned to persevere until I really understand or achieve something. I embrace creative problem-solving strategies, think outside the box, and try new activities or create new ways of doing things. Plus, I've developed empathy with others who learn differently.

These strengths have enabled and equipped me to be aware of my students' diverse needs, and I work to meet those needs by presenting content in different ways and letting students share their learning in a multitude of ways. Even though the standards guide my instruction, nothing about how I teach is standardized. It's dynamic and different—like my learners. I'll share much more about what I offer to students with diverse needs in the section about kinesthetic lessons.

I'm also a better learner because of dyslexia. Ironically, I use many of the strategies I've learned in my education coursework not only to enhance my students' knowledge, but also to develop personal comprehension and critical thinking skills I didn't develop as a nonreader.

As difficult as my obstacles were to overcome, the strengths I've developed and the person I've become because of them definitely justify the effort. Would we really wish for an easy life when our greatest learning comes through overcoming obstacles? Though I didn't always feel this way, I developed the courage and positivity to be grateful for my life—obstacles and all—through perseverance. I believe we should be celebrating the opportunities our obstacles provide. My goal is to share ways we can push through our obstacles to elevate us to new levels of personal greatness.

Flex Your EduNinja Muscles

★ What are some obstacles you have faced?

★ How can your obstacles be a strength or advantage?

★ How can you encourage students to see their weaknesses as learning opportunities?

★ How can you better connect with your students' interests in music, sports, or art and incorporate those into lessons?

★ How can you set the bar higher for your students?

An EduNinja
Is Reflective
and Protective

When we know better, we do better.

—Maya Angelou

*Your own self-realization is the greatest
service you can render the world.*

—Ramana Maharshi

*You can't connect the dots looking forward;
you can only connect them looking backwards.*

—Steve Jobs

On our journey to personal greatness, it's important to spend time in purposeful activities to slow down, truly check in with ourselves, and regain focus. Part of the EduNinja Mindset is being self-aware, and I've discovered journaling is an empowering tool to use for this. A regular, reflective writing routine helps us engage with our feelings, ask questions about the story behind the feelings, and connect the dots between thoughts and behaviors. Sometimes we're "so busy" we lose our focus and overlook the very things we need in order to be happy. Journaling is a great way to slow down and ask ourselves questions in a nonjudgmental way. It also gives us a safe, egoless, truthful environment in which to courageously answer.

Journaling allows you to shed your armor, drop the lie you may have been telling yourself, and face things you may have been avoiding through numbing activities. For example, maybe you didn't realize you were overeating, binge-TV-watching, or social surfing in an effort to mask or avoid thinking about very important feelings and actions. Journaling helps you look for patterns in your life and behaviors, strengthen your ideas, and develop new ones so you can learn more about yourself and the world around you. This proactive, regular reflection also helps you take advantage of opportunities and make strong choices based on your values. Doing this ensures you're living an authentic, happy, and meaningful life.

But I'm Not a Writer

Many of you may identify with me when I say I wasn't a writer. But my life is more abundant and meaningful since I started journaling. The key is to start; regular journaling gets easier with purposeful practice. Write a daily reflection or blog or create a "gratitude journal" or a place to build future ideas. Journaling can take on a range of forms, but the point of writing is that it helps you slow down to mindfully notice your emotions, thinking, and behaviors making up your complete story. Then, you can come up with strategies to create a better ending. And if you like talking with friends about what's on your mind, do both—writing *and* sharing—as an opportunity to learn about yourself and develop new ideas.

I discovered I needed to stay as consistent in my journal writing as I was with my fitness routine. I write for ten to fifteen minutes before going to bed. Even a small amount of time in reflective writing exercises shows me when my current situation isn't aligned to my core values, which forces me to dig deep, look my emotions in the eye, and make needed changes to elevate to another level. Daily reflection and journal writing can easily become part of your routine too. You'll gain confidence each day, noticing strong emotions, asking yourself tough questions, and facing those emotions by considering what they're really saying about your thoughts and actions.

What do you have to lose by writing ten minutes a day? Start now by setting a reminder on your phone, making a commitment to your Professional Learning Network (PLN) on Twitter, or creating a self-reflecting journaling group at school. Start a blog or blogging group to connect virtually or meet with friends personally to share your reflective questions or blog ideas. This practice may become a game changer for you. It was for me.

I Can't Think of Anything to Write

Have you ever given your students a writing assignment only to hear, "I can't think of anything to write"? Likely you've discovered giving them a writing prompt gets their brains (and pens) going. The same is true for journaling. If you don't know where to start, use one of these prompts to spark some ideas:

- I notice …
- I wonder why …
- This makes me think …
- On one hand …
- On the other hand …
- I learned …

- I used to think … and now I think …
- My future self will thank me for …

We often use prompts like these in our classrooms, but we rarely use them in our personal lives. However, they will help us become acute observers of life. As you write, take time to notice things and make connections. For example, I discovered *several* things about myself in this journal entry:

> I notice when I go to bed earlier, I feel better, I'm in a better mood. I have more energy for teaching engaging lessons. This makes me think I should set a bedtime alarm so I'm at my best and my energy levels stay connected throughout the day. I also notice I love the taste of lattes and the quick energy surge of an espresso in the morning, but I feel so much better when I drink green tea because it reduces the extreme energy highs and lows. Similarly, even though I don't always feel like exercising, I always feel better when I've worked out. My EduNinja mindset propels me to the gym, allowing my effort to take over and the endorphins to kick in! When all aspects of my life are balanced, I'm at my personal best to serve the people who need me.

These small "noticings" of events and patterns over time, whether they are emotional, physical, or both, help us make purposeful choices instead of being passive and letting life just happen. As you journal, you'll be amazed at how good you get at noticing things, creating connections, and making decisions aligned to what you want and need.

In addition to prompts, you can also base your writing on and around a number of other elements. Consider any of these to inspire your reflective writing exercises.

- close observations
- questions
- reflections about what you see, hear, or think
- favorite quotes
- dreams
- new ideas you want to explore
- inquiry-based questions about an interesting topic
- family stories
- goals you want to achieve
- conflicts you want to resolve
- pros and cons of decisions you need to make
- create lists of things you want in your life, places you want to travel, your passion projects, and things you care deeply about
- objects to sketch
- words for wordplay
- writing a letter—maybe even to yourself

Setting Boundaries

Reflective writing may help you discover you need to put yourself first at times in order to best meet your needs. After my divorce, I realized putting my partner's needs first wasn't healthy; I had lost practice noticing my own needs. Sometimes we neglect putting our needs first because we don't want to let others down, hurt their feelings, or see them struggle with something we could do for them. Or maybe you're wondering how you could possibly put yourself first when you have a family to take care of. But the reality is that when you're at your best, you are better able to care for your family. Think about the preflight safety demonstrations: "Secure your mask first, then assist the other person." But to be your best, you need to make some time for *you*.

Putting your needs first is equally important, both at home and in the classroom. We teachers fly through our days, sometimes forgetting to drink water, use the restroom, or get out of our classroom to see other adults. We often come in for early meetings, prepare lessons during our lunch breaks, and stay after school to help students. Those are qualities of a great teacher, right? Not always. Have you ever considered you may be working so hard to serve your students you're neglecting your own needs? As a result, you may become less effective in the classroom and develop burnout.

Healthy habits positively affect mood and performance, but developing and sustaining those habits can be challenging. Even with almost twenty years of elementary teaching experience, I still struggle to maintain the right work-life balance to sustain optimum energy levels for the entire year. However, this past year I regularly practiced noticing and listening to my needs during the day and developed proactive strategies to prevent burnout. I'm happy to say this led to my personal best year of teaching. My workload tripled due to passion projects like leading professional development workshops for teachers, writing this book, starting EduNinja™ Fit, helping to facilitate a health and wellness program at our school, and starting the planning for EduNinja nonprofit, but my effectiveness and engagement in school lessons increased. By consistently practicing health and wellness strategies for myself and my students, student engagement and focus increased.

This positive shift came when I learned to set some boundaries to provide time for *me*. Sometimes we just need to slow down and refine our ability to recognize the signs of imbalance piling up over a sustained period of time. Neglecting proactive work-life balance strategies can easily—and negatively—impact our classroom community.

So how do we set boundaries for ourselves? Practice noticing your feelings and your responses. For example, if you're getting angry or upset, ask yourself if there is a boundary you need to set. If you're concerned about feeling guilty for agreeing to something, try saying, "Can I get back to you on that?" Practice putting yourself first by scheduling time each day for you. Honor your time and keep your appointment no matter what obstacles arise.

Setting and sustaining healthy boundaries is a skill. When you need to set a boundary, try rehearsing. Confidently say your boundary without any excuses or the word "but" because it weakens your power. Be specific and set a timeframe for what needs to change. Know what to do or assertively say when people don't respect your boundary. Ask them to stop immediately. There is no need to give in to guilt trippers, temper tantrums, or manipulation. Do not engage in any negative comments that may arise from them. Trust yourself. Finally, don't be afraid to delegate or say "no thanks" if something doesn't align to your values.

My favorite part about setting boundaries is acknowledging and thanking those who are supporting and respecting your personal boundaries. It will most likely encourage them to continue the positive behaviors. The more you practice maintaining healthy boundaries, the more love, respect, and support you will find in your life. As teachers we are fortunate to get lots of practice.

Flex Your EduNinja Muscles

Grab a notebook and start journaling. Answer these questions to get started:

- ★ How and when do you create space to listen to your thoughts?

- ★ Do you set aside daily time to practice journaling? If not, what's getting in the way?

- ★ What supports do you need to refine your practice?

- ★ Who could help you grow your practice and help you develop accountability?

- ★ What activities or restorative practices (i.e., yoga, journaling, hiking, massages) refuel you?

- ★ Do you schedule time to take care of your needs first? If so, how often?

- ★ Do you honor the time you schedule for yourself without letting other obligations take up the time? What helps you commit to your schedule?

- ★ What boundary "pitfalls" do you potentially see at different times of the school year? What proactive strategies could you put in place to avoid these?

An EduNinja
Sets Goals with Soul

*If we are willing to stand fully in our own shoes
and never give up on ourselves, then we will
be able to put ourselves in the shoes of
others and never give up on them.*

—Pema Chödrön, *Start Where You Are:
A Guide to Compassionate Living*

You're likely wondering what a five-foot-two-inch girl—who *failed* to finish the *American Ninja Warrior* course—has to say about goal-setting. Why should you listen to me? Because I haven't finished the course ... *yet!* Hitting the famous Ninja Warrior red button was my "goal with soul." But just because I missed the goal once or twice doesn't mean the goal is forever out of reach. Missing a goal is exactly where learning begins.

I wasn't always a ninja. I didn't always set big goals in all areas of my life. Maybe like you, I found it easier to set big goals in the areas of my life where I was already succeeding. But I rarely took the time to cultivate my whole being and develop the areas not working for me. One thing my success on *America Ninja Warrior* taught me (yes, I said *success*) is that life is simply a series of setting and resetting goals. We set a goal, miss it, reset, try again, reset, try again, hit the goal, and raise the bar to a higher goal. You don't have to love the work you put into achieving a goal, but you do have to be passionate about your goal if you want to be successful. Goals with soul are the ones giving you purpose, the ones you stay focused on, the ones giving you vision even when things get tough. If you set a superficial goal, you may experience short-term success, but most likely it won't fulfill or sustain you.

So set goals you love. Take time to explore areas of your life needing deeper work. Is there one area you keep trying to "fix" but aren't having the success you'd like? Look for the underlying belief limiting your success. We all have at least one area we can dig into and set bigger goals for. What is yours? You don't need to wait for a life-altering event to gain the courage to set bigger goals.

Identify focused, long-term SMART—Specific, Measurable, Achievable, Relevant, and Time-Bound—goals and commit to achieving them. You will benefit if you set daily, weekly, monthly, yearly, five-year, ten-year, and lifetime goals. Also, set goals in multiple areas of your life: school/professional, family, spiritual, health/wellness. Create your weekly schedule of SMART goals each Sunday and align these goals to eventually meet your long-term goals with soul.

Base Your Goals on Core Values

Before doing any type of goal-setting, it's important to explore your core values. Otherwise, your goals may be superficial, sound like everyone else's, lack meaning and purpose, and be harder to reach. What big themes and beliefs have always been important to you? These are the deep and lasting threads in your life, the beliefs you know to be true no matter what situation you are in or what people are around you. If you don't do the reflective work to identify your values and define them in order of their importance, you may be easily influenced by others. Instead of purposefully working to achieve the goals you value and believe in, you may become a passive reactor to others' requests of you. If we "get real" with ourselves and our needs, the goals we set today will be meaningful, sustainable, and possibly life-changing.

By clearly identifying and defining your core values, you'll be able to make easier decisions in all areas of your life because you will choose what aligns with your values. Decisions about how to spend your time, effort, and money will all be easier when they are made with your core values in mind. Consider the following questions as you spend time brainstorming, identifying, and clarifying your values:

- Who are your important mentors? What core qualities about them are inspiring?
- Think about a time you were in the "flow," feeling an effortless peak performance, or experiencing one of your greatest accomplishments. What core beliefs helped you succeed?
- What are some of the biggest failures you learned from? What core values helped you through these?
- When have you felt "off track" and why? What did you need at that time? Are those needs being met today? What can you do differently to succeed when these experiences arise again?
- What qualities do you want to cultivate? What can you do to learn? Who can help?

Make a list of five to ten core values to help guide your time, energy, and decision-making and order them by importance. See if you can combine or eliminate any. Write about the top two or three, describing in-depth how or why these are important in your life. How are they integrated into your life, or how or where can they be better integrated? Some areas you may want to include are personal growth, balanced healthy habits, lasting relationships, or passion for service.

When students write stories, we teach them to look at their values and develop a message they want to teach others. You can do the same. Make a list of the potential big themes or important life lessons you'd want to share with others if you were writing a story. Some I've identified are the following:

- Never stop learning.
- Be humble.
- Be kind.
- Surround yourself with people who will make you better.
- Show gratitude daily.
- Live life with passion and purpose.
- Share your unique gifts and try to enhance the lives of others.
- Build deeper connections and meaningful relationships to enhance your life.

Be Your Own Cheerleader

While working on overall goals, it's important to keep a positive mindset. Otherwise, we might allow ourselves to hear discouraging or defeating messages, preventing us from growing and achieving our goals. As I continued to develop my reflective writing habit, I began trusting I was in the right place in life. But I also knew if I wanted to grow, I had to take new risks and new actions. As a lifelong athlete, I wanted to be a healthy role model to inspire others and mentor athletes at all levels and ages. More importantly, I wanted to listen to my inner voice and act in ways reflecting the best version of me.

To encourage my inner voice to stay positive, I started leaving notes for myself in my journal. Notes like "I am extraordinary" or

"Yes I can" continually clarified and helped me build the life I wanted in the future. At first some of these words seemed uncomfortable. One note I'd written said, "I am loved, I am loveable, I am healed, I am whole," but it didn't resonate with me because I had never talked to myself this way before. But over time, these words became more comfortable. Hearing and seeing them daily helped me turn down the critical dial in my head. Instead of hearing, "You'll never get everything on your list done" or "Don't go for it—you're not good enough," I was reprogramming my inner voice to say, "Celebrate your small victories!" or "You're strong and capable!" I became my own cheerleader.

Reading these positive notes regularly helped build a positive mindset. I knew I deserved to offer and receive love freely, regardless of the situation I was in. We owe it to ourselves to ignore made-up stories—the ones saying we aren't good enough or we're not deserving—as well as the untruths seemingly protecting us from the potential pain of failure, yet holding us back in the process.

Setting bigger goals is challenging if you don't believe you are good enough. But once you believe you're worthy, you'll be able to set bigger goals and authentically stand in your truth. We're awesome cheerleaders for our students, telling them, "You've got this!" or "You're going to crush this!" or "Don't stop until you are proud!" or "Mistakes are proof you're trying!" Why wouldn't we cheer for ourselves in the same way? We need to say positive things to empower ourselves, especially when it feels no one else is encouraging us.

The more you practice positive self-talk, the more you'll catch yourself thanking and celebrating your students, friends, and loved ones. Expressing authentic gratitude builds trust and strengthens relationships because the more connected you are, the more committed you become.

One way to add more positive self-talk is to flip some of your current thoughts. For example, instead of saying that being short was a disadvantage in volleyball or that I had difficulty reading, writing, or public speaking, I learned to say, "Because of my height, I may be quicker to dig volleyballs" or "I can talk and write about my difficulties with reading, writing, and public speaking to help others, which, ironically, helps me strengthen these skills." Instead of saying you have difficulty understanding multi-step directions, say, "I listen closely so I can ask better clarifying questions. I then break the directions into more manageable steps."

Make Personal Promises

Many of you may remember the early 1990s Saturday Night Live skits where Stuart Smalley shared his daily affirmations with the world: "I'm good enough, I'm smart enough, and, doggone it, people like me!" This skit was the only context I had for personal promises until I tried writing my own. In a pre-*Ninja Warrior* journal entry, I wrote:

> In 2012 I seize this moment. I choose now to create the life of my dreams by reconnecting with the highest aspect of myself, being the best version of me, and doing the next right thing. I will no longer spend my time listening to doubt, fear, or negative thinking.

I'd written this promise based on my needs, not selected from a book, and I read it every day for strength. It was exactly what I needed to implement daily bits of courage, and I knew, eventually, I would feel comfortable saying these words. At the time, I had to grow into the words by continuing to tackle small daily fears. But with this mindset, I knew I had the strength to keep learning, growing, and pushing past my comfort zones. Personal promises proactively tell us what to aspire to. Instead of listening to doubt, fear, and made-up stories, personal promises give us strength, perseverance, courage, radical trust, and love, and they elevate us to a new level.

Later in 2012 I wrote "My October Mantra" to clarify and refine my new vision:

> *I'm inspired to develop beyond my previously self-imposed limits to coordinate my mind and my body to the point where my confidence overrides my fears.*

I made this commitment to myself in order to gain strength and courage from the inside out, and to accomplish goals I had been too afraid to set before. For the majority of my life, I had been extremely shy, afraid to speak up, and fearful of addressing important issues in order to please others. "My October Mantra" was the foundational change in my thinking, and it positively impacted the rest of my life. I made this promise to myself—to set goals with soul, to keep going, to push forward by putting myself in situations where I felt uncomfortable, to push through obstacles, to reflect, and to keep moving forward. It was my promise to talk when I needed to, instead of staying quiet, shy, and afraid, and to have tough conversations when something didn't align with my values. By pushing through the uncomfortable moments, I was able to slowly develop strength.

When you write your own personal promises, first identify your need(s):

I need _____

Second, restate your need in a positive statement. I've included some templates you can try, or you can make your own.

I will _____ by_____.

I am_____ because_____.

I love_____ because_____.

I'm inspired to _____ by _____.

Digging deep to identify my needs, creating a personal promise I could grow into, and reading it daily were the first small steps in tackling my fears and developing a new mindset. Personal promises don't magically come true, but they are strong verbal reminders of what we'd like to create. We're often reminded about the power of words and the need to choose them wisely. We need to develop a plan, take courageous steps, and maintain steadfast determination in practicing and refining our goals.

Flex Your EduNinja Muscles

★ What SMART goals will you achieve today? This week? This month? In five or ten years?

★ What are your *goals with soul* and how will you begin to achieve them?

★ What words do you need to hear?

★ What are some favorite words your mentors tell you? What are some of your favorite positive phrases? How and where can you share those words and phrases more often?

★ In what area of your life could you use a positive personal promise? Create one and say it daily. Put it on your computer, bathroom mirror, or near your coffee maker and see what happens.

An EduNinja
Lives on Purpose

I n 2012, I met an opportunity to change my life and thrive—not just cope. Jolted by a divorce, I was forced to reevaluate my core values to ensure they were truly in line with *my* beliefs, without being influenced by anyone else. I wanted to strengthen my foundation to ensure I was aligning my future actions with my values and practicing them daily.

I started paying attention to the very small, moment-to-moment choices I was making, and I began to see how these choices created patterns or trends in my behavior. Being divorced provided more time and fewer distractions, giving me the opportunity to practice mindful observation. As I created time, space, and mindfulness, I noticed these purposefully applied strategies produced positive results, such as greater clarity. I developed a reflective and introspective routine of venturing out on nightly three-hour urban hikes, building the foundation to my new mindset. I followed this "mindful movement" with reading and journaling, helping me reflect on where I was in my life and what I wanted next.

What Are You Training For?

While working out at a local gym in Orwigsburg during Thanksgiving break, I met Matt, a fellow Nittany Lion who had played football at Penn State and was substitute teaching, hoping to get picked up as a free agent. He asked me, "What are you training for?" After thinking for a moment, I replied, "Life." Matt had asked a simple question, but it prompted me to consider finding a bigger purpose to train for.

As fellow athletes, neither of us could turn down the opportunity to share our workouts instead of working out alone. So when Matt offered to take me through a football weightlifting workout the following day, I reciprocated on the third day with high intensity interval training with bodyweight exercises. We discovered we had both grown up in Orwigsburg and attended the same high school. We had similar athletic dispositions and dedication—and we both had dyslexia!

I was impressed with Matt's passion for sharing his training, and I found taking him through my workout highly rewarding. A lifelong friendship was born during those few days at the gym, inspiring me to elevate my life. Matt gave me a copy of *The Alchemist* by Paulo Coelho, which I had read previously. However, rereading it was transformative as I rediscovered some of the life-defining quotes:

- Life is really generous to those that pursue their personal legend.
- When a person really desires something, all the universe conspires to help that person to realize his dream.
- Wherever your heart is, there you will find your treasure.
- It's the possibility of having a dream come true that makes life interesting.

These words resonated with me and inspired me to live more fully and passionately and find my deeper life purpose. I knew I had a strong knowledge base and passion for training across sports and with different types of athletes. I determined I wanted to build on my knowledge and passion and pursue the deeper purpose of coaching others to discover their own personal greatness. I realized I needed to train with purpose, compete at a higher level, and share these training strategies with others, but I still didn't know how to answer Matt's question: *What are you training for?*

"The Call"

In early January after meeting Matt, I returned to Pennsylvania again for a Penn State alumni volleyball event and scrimmage. During our game, after I dove and rolled for a ball, my former teammate said, "Burd, you play volleyball like a ninja. You need to be on *American Ninja Warrior!*"

At that moment, I thought of the resolution I had made just before this trip about inspiring people on a bigger level. *American Ninja Warrior* would be an opportunity to put this into action. When I shared my resolution with another college teammate, she said I needed to add the word "greatness." Initially, I thought "greatness" sounded too bold, but I realized we should all be striving to achieve greatness. So my new resolution became: "I want to inspire greatness on a bigger level."

When I got home, *The Alchemist* quotes resonating with my new goals, I quickly applied for *American Ninja Warrior*, only telling a handful of people. Two weeks later, I got "the call," finally feeling I was fulfilling the greater purpose to inspire people on a bigger level, beyond the walls of my classroom. I was combining a purpose-driven, passionate goal with reflective writing, thinking about inspirational, positive quotes, and fully listening to others, finding ways to share my talents to help them in my unique way. I finally felt everything coming together in a positive, passionate, reflective, purposeful, and supportive way. This fueled my passion and ignited my teaching. I had found a way to creatively combine the two.

Stating Your Mission

I now had a purpose. I could answer Matt's question about what I was training for. Now it was time to write a mission statement. When I originally created a personal mission statement for my website, I didn't realize how life changing the process would be. The act of defining, writing, and regularly seeing my mission statement acted as a self-fulfilling prophecy. I wholeheartedly believed every word. My mission statement was truly driving my actions and decisions about how and why I was spending time: I was in pursuit of helping others reach their personal greatness.

You'll see my mission statement on jenburdis.com:

Inspiring greatness on a bigger level by encouraging people to live a passionate, healthy lifestyle, become the best version of themselves, overcome obstacles, set goals, work hard, and make a positive difference in the lives of others.

Over time I realized this was my *personal* mission statement, but I didn't have a professional mission. So I developed a professional mission statement aimed at serving and inspiring teachers and students to live healthier:

Building the foundation of sound nutrition, movement, and mindfulness to meet the needs of teachers, students, and families.

The process of writing these mission statements—from crafting the words, feeling them, seeing them regularly, saying them, and refining them—helped me align my core values and live them authentically, purposefully, and with passion. Because the process had been so rewarding, I knew I could also benefit from creating a family mission statement:

> I want to be the best daughter, aunt, and sister by adding value to my loved ones' lives, showing gratitude and love often by planning consistent quality times to connect.

As teachers, we do reverse planning, looking at the end date of a unit and planning backwards. We can use this same strategy in our own lives as we identify our purpose and write our mission statements. Think about the following questions as you consider your own purpose and mission:

- If you were to write an autobiography, how would you want it to end?
- In order to avoid any regrets at the end of your life, what things do you want to accomplish? What do you wish people would say about you?
- What does personal greatness look like to you? What does it look like in your relationships? In your job?
- Are your current day-to-day habits getting you closer to your life mission? If not, what changes need to be made?
- Think about if you won the lottery or retired. How would you fill your days? What are you passionate about? How can you connect your passion and purpose?

Take a look at the top five values you identified earlier and create a personal mission statement to help guide and align your passion and purpose to better serve others. Words have tremendous power. Seeing them, saying them, hearing them, and truly believing them may become a self-fulfilling prophecy for you too. Choose your words wisely as you craft your personal mission statement to blend your purpose, talents, values, and passion. Consider making a mission statement for different areas of your life, such as personal, professional, and family. Does one mission statement supersede them all?

How do you go from creating a mission statement to living it? Education leader Todd Whitaker says, "Don't tell the world your mission statement. Show the world you are on a mission." Here are some practical tips to help you do this:

- Ask yourself daily if your activities align with your mission statement.
- Create time to reflect in your journal or blog.
- Connect with others who are on the same mission. Learn from, support, and encourage one another.
- Collaborate with others in different fields to connect to a bigger vision and learn from them.
- Stay positive when adversity strikes, obstacles appear, and failure occurs.

If you need a reminder of why we need a mission statement to help us become all we're capable of being, make a T-chart. On the left-hand side, list all the positive things related to trying to reach your personal mission. On the right-hand side, write down the things you'll experience if you don't step up and go for it. These lists will likely be sobering—and motivating.

Flex Your EduNinja Muscles

★ How do your core values tie into your higher purpose?

★ Is teaching your higher purpose? Why do you teach?

★ How do you want to live? What does the best version of you look like?

★ Think about your unique talents. Are you tapping into them fully to help others?

★ Is there a way you can creatively combine your talents, passion, and vocation to help others?

An EduNinja
Embraces Imperfection

5

*We don't need to be perfect. Let the ego go,
ditch the pride and the protective strategies, and
just have the courage to be your true authentic self.
What makes you vulnerable makes you beautiful.*

—Brené Brown

*We're all imperfect and we all have needs.
The weak usually do not ask for help, so they
stay weak. If we recognize that we are imperfect,
we will ask for help and we will pray for the
guidance necessary to bring positive results
to whatever we are doing.*

—John Wooden

*Those who dare to fail miserably
can achieve greatly.*

—John F. Kennedy

I t was 4:30 a.m., and I was about to step up onto the *American Ninja Warrior* platform for the second time. But I didn't feel as confident as I had as a rookie. Physically, I felt more prepared; I'd been training for an entire year. But mentally, I was stressed. Report cards, parent conferences, and a lack of support for missing school to run the course, combined with the crazy timing of closing on the sale of my house and moving, were weighing on me. While I didn't specifically think about those things while I was on the platform, I was uncertain of the strategies needed to get through the upcoming obstacles. My plan and visualization weren't clear. My mindset wasn't in check.

When I got the green light to start my run, I bounded confidently and successfully through the five massive steps, feeling no fear as I replicated something I'd trained for and was proficient in. But as I pulled myself up the platform to face my next obstacle, I knew it was one I'd never tried before. Picture this: you've borrowed long cloth curtains from your grandma's house and looped them around a pipe, leaving the ends hanging down about three feet on both ends of the pipe. You have to grab the curtains, push yourself off a platform and try to create enough momentum to fly down and out and launch yourself through the air far enough to grab a suspended rope with both hands and swing across to the next platform—all while a bungee, attached to the pipe, is trying to pull you backwards.

I stood on my tiptoes to reach the red silk slider cloth. Unfortunately, I wasn't able to generate enough force from my toes to push off the platform as aggressively as I wanted. As a result, I was moving in what seemed like slow motion, sliding dreadfully and slowly down the slanted pipe without the momentum I needed to launch and catch the rope. One of my hands barely touched the rope before my full year of training two-a-days got washed up as my body hit the water, and the red light and buzzer confirmed my *American Ninja Warrior* run was abruptly over. I was crushed.

Falling on the second obstacle left me completely devastated, vulnerable, and wanting to quit. This was the biggest disappointment of my entire athletic life. In other sports, I'd had the next game to look forward to or the next race to train for. With *American Ninja Warrior*, I'd spent a full committed year of training, ripping my hands and falling more than I could possibly count. A year's worth of training, and I only got a short burst on the course. It was a brutal feeling, but there were big lessons to learn. A major shift in my thinking began to take place.

I understood before running the course that if we truly push ourselves to attempt something new and unpracticed, we increase our risk of failing. And I knew failure is ultimately feedback, helping us figure out what we can do differently to prepare for the next opportunity. But I didn't want to continue this *American Ninja Warrior* journey. I had felt mildly successful in my first *Ninja* run in season six because my performance matched my rookie training. I could easily look at it as a learning opportunity. But season seven's performance stung a lot!

Just Out of Reach

About this time, one of my ninja friends Sam Sann called me and said, "Jen, what would your students think if you just gave up after this? It's important you keep going. It's important for them to learn this lesson from you."

But how do we face fears, go for it, fail miserably, and become comfortable with doing it all over again? We flip the script and simply change our mindset. As I changed mine, I realized season seven of the *American Ninja Warrior* offered me a different learning opportunity than season six had. As I replayed grasping the silk slider with one hand while missing the rope transfer, I began to think, *Shouldn't all of our goals be just out of reach?* We tell our students to set goals just barely within or just beyond their reach. Why shouldn't it be the same for us? Our goals aren't big enough if we reach all of them. I needed to rise above to succeed, and this became my new focus.

After taking almost a month off to let my body recover from negotiating obstacles, and letting the sting of my failure subside, I started my parkour training of running up walls, vaulting, and precision jumping again. On a Sunday in May of 2015, I was ready to be running routes again. I passed a young boy wearing a cast and on a scooter. I easily remember my words to him: "It's all about the risk and reward in this sport." I didn't realize at the time, as I was getting ready to make my last run of the day to beat my time on the course, how true those words were.

I handed my phone to a parkour classmate and asked if he would shoot a video of my last run. Little did I know, only seconds later he would be recording me as I tore my left Achilles. As I sprinted full force, the heel of my left foot hit the inclined wall with a memorable noise as my Achilles ripped and my foot flopped onto the floor. Even though I hoped for a twisted ankle, there was no doubt what had happened. As I felt the back of my ankle, my hand sank into a huge divot just above my heel. I hobbled to the car, put an ice pack on it, and drove home, still hoping to "sleep it off" and wake up to just an ankle sprain.

Not What I Planned

The following morning, a physician assistant confirmed my Achilles was torn and hanging on "just enough" that I could let it heal instead of having surgery. I was grateful to hear his recommendation even though I knew letting it heal naturally would take longer and the re-rupture rate would be higher. But I wouldn't have to have surgery.

My foot was casted, and I was given crutches. This was the beginning of what would become a two-year recovery process.

Clearly, I wouldn't be running another *American Ninja Warrior* course any time soon. I thought of what Sam had told me, and I was disappointed and frustrated my students weren't going to see me come back and compete again after my failed second run. In addition, I found myself in an unfamiliar situation. My regular routines had been completely disrupted, and I wasn't able to be as self-sufficient as I was used to being. I had to learn to be okay with being vulnerable, and be willing to ask for and accept help from others.

For starters, I had to have help moving all my things downstairs from my bedroom, and I lived on the first floor for over a year. My days began a half hour earlier so I could manage my morning routine, including the challenge of trying to make breakfast—moving across the kitchen on crutches while trying to hold a cereal bowl, getting the milk out of the fridge, and balancing on my uncasted foot while I poured it. Luckily, I could drive with my right foot, but getting in and out of my car with my school bags was a challenge, and teaching was difficult because I couldn't touch my casted foot to the ground.

For months, I moved everywhere with crutches. I transitioned out of the cast after the first month and into a boot but still wasn't able to touch it to the ground. My foot had to be held like an injured baby bird because it couldn't move on its own. The toes wouldn't move even when I told them to as I gently lifted my foot in or out of the boot.

After the first few months, I could eventually touch the booted foot to the ground, but I wasn't allowed to do any exercise on it. I had been overtraining my upper body with pull-ups, rowing, and lifting but, because I developed tendonitis in my right elbow during the first month using crutches, I went from training multiple hours a day, to training just my upper body, to training zero hours a day. My new workouts consisted only of challenging toe flexion exercises. As I was retraining my brain from this injury, I had to relearn how to wiggle my toes, and how to walk on my left foot by taking baby steps again.

Imperfect Is Okay

During my recovery, I had been meeting and growing my professional network of teachers and, coincidentally, connected with another Penn State student athlete, Adam Taliaferro, who offered support from time to time with a Twitter message. Adam was a Penn State football player who had been seriously injured while making a tackle in a game against Ohio State in 2000. After spinal-fusion surgery, doctors had told Adam he had a 3 percent chance to walk again. With hard work and a positive mindset, Adam miraculously walked out of his hospital only three months later. Currently, Adam's nonprofit foundation lends a helping hand to individuals who have suffered life-altering spinal injuries. Adam is a living example of turning obstacles into strengths, and he helped me change my perspective about my own obstacles.

I originally had a timeline in my head of when I should have been able to walk again, based on some information my physician assistant had given me. Plus, everyone I talked to who had torn their Achilles said they were back to activities in six months. I was disappointed, then, when I wasn't able to start taking baby steps on my own until after four months. I wondered how someone like Adam, paralyzed and given a 3 percent chance of walking, had walked out of the hospital when I couldn't even take a few steps on my carpeted living room floor after a torn Achilles.

Adam reminded me of all the people who would never be able to walk again, and I realized a torn Achilles is nothing by comparison. Adam helped me shift my thinking, and I felt compassion for those suffering lifelong spinal cord and other debilitating injuries. I immediately thought how grateful I was to be able to walk and run again eventually, even if it wasn't at the same level. I was becoming okay with not being "perfect."

I started celebrating slow gains. I looked at my recovery from a new perspective, reframing each negative situation into an opportunity. If I hadn't torn my Achilles, I never would have made meaningful Twitter friendships in my Professional Learning Network, taken time for creative outlets and reflection, and wouldn't have written this book. Because I was open and willing, I started to merge my passions of lifelong learning, building connections, teaching, and offering health and wellness coaching. I also noticed there wasn't a lot of support for our teachers, despite their having one of the most important jobs in the country, and I started looking at how I could help them add value to what they do.

During this time, I met inspiring individuals who helped guide me to new and exciting professional challenges. Sean Galliard, #EdBeat founder, nudged me to guest moderate my first Twitter chat with this supportive educational tribe. The Grundler's #k12artchat accepted me, a general education teacher, showing me the value of creating every day, and nudged me to participate in Tim Needle's 30 Day #TERPArt Challenge. Together we created art, discovered new apps, and shared our learning. Individuals in these communities believed in me, supported me, pushed me, and gave me confidence to share my learning.

Overcoming Disappointment

Physically, I was now overweight, soft, and weak. All my hard work from the previous years had vanished in a few months. My left calf muscle atrophied to mush, staying "smooshed" when I pinched it. Without working out for two years, my whole body felt like someone else's. Hip and back problems emerged, and I had major imbalances from wearing the boot for so long. I spent two full years trying—and failing—to do assisted independent calf raises before I could finally do a left calf raise on my own.

But, as challenging as my physical situation was, without tearing my Achilles, I wouldn't have carved out the reflective time needed to think about what's really important to aligning my passions and purpose. Before my injury, I thought serving the students in my class was enough. But I realized I could tap into a higher level of service by interacting with experts, refining what I was doing in my class, and encouraging other teachers by giving them the tools I was using to learn and grow. Before my tear, I thought I was too busy to add anything to my plate. In reality, I just needed time to slow down, make a plan, and accept the guidance of positive leaders. During my Achilles rehab, I practiced the EduNinja Mindset by putting myself in new, challenging situations. It wasn't an easy two years, but just because I couldn't walk didn't mean I couldn't keep moving forward.

> **It wasn't an easy two years, but just because I couldn't walk didn't mean I couldn't keep moving forward.**

As we push to work at higher levels and take on new projects, which at first glance may seem out of our range, inevitably we are going to fail—and sometimes fail hard. But the EduNinja Mindset gives us the drive, courage, and passion to believe the unbelievable and try anyway—knowing we're going to fail, fail big, and fail often. Failure is encouraged and accepted in the EduNinja community because we know this is the only way to grow. Surround yourself with

EduNinjas who will cheer you on as you attempt new obstacles, fall, and get back up to do it all over again.

Michelle Obama captured this idea of resilience beautifully when she said:

> It's easy to get A's. What happens when you fail? When you work as hard as you can and you don't reach your goal? What do you do? Do you fall apart? Do you quit? Do you beat yourself up? Or do you get up and keep working a little bit harder? That's what success is. That is the ultimate quality of a successful person. It is resilience. It is the ability to overcome obstacles.

The people you consider to be the most successful have likely failed more times than you have. Social media tends to highlight the happy and successful, and sometimes even forces a perception of success or people having it all figured out. But if you could see more closely, you'd see they have their own version of the hands and bodies of *American Ninja Warrior* athletes—ripped open and calloused hands, bruised bodies, and pulled muscles. You would know the road to overcoming a single obstacle didn't come without bouts of failure. Be an EduNinja. Take risks. Understand that perspective is the key. Failure is the clearest way to see what we need to work on. Be resilient and bounce back. Set a plan, gather supportive people, and get to work.

Being Vulnerable

Vulnerability is an integral part of taking risks and learning from failure. To be vulnerable is to be emotionally exposed—to let people see your "imperfection." Vulnerability shows up in our lives in different ways. What's emotionally exposing and scary for one person may be a strength or opportunity for someone else. For example, only a couple of weeks after I submitted my *American Ninja Warrior* video, I got "the call" and was told I could tell my class. I sprinted into the classroom next door where my students were in class with my team teacher and hijacked her lesson, asking if I could tell them something. When I blurted out, "I'm going to be on *American Ninja Warrior!*" the students exploded into screams. After the cheering and celebrating stopped, I could barely wait for the three o'clock bell to ring so I could run off to share the exciting news with my colleagues.

The second teacher I shared my news with looked at me with wide open eyes and exclaimed, "That would be my worst nightmare! No joke." *What?* That wasn't the answer I was expecting at all. Where else do you get to stand on a huge, brightly lit platform with adrenaline coursing through your veins as you sprint across quintuple steps or wrap your body around an accelerating spinning log with the hope of getting flung off onto the mat so you can run up and leap off a mini trampoline to grab onto the next obstacle as the crowd cheers you on?! Who wouldn't want to do this? I couldn't quite wrap my head around why she'd think this experience would be a nightmare.

This same teacher had confidently dressed up as "Bryan" from *Koo Koo Kanga Roo* to emcee our kindergarten through fifth grade dance party, raised her hand confidently in staff meetings to ask tough questions, and proudly declared when she didn't understand something. How could *American Ninja Warrior* be her worst nightmare? I started thinking how scared and vulnerable I'd feel to say even one line in front of the whole school or raise my hand at a staff meeting to say I didn't understand something. Obviously, I hadn't been setting the bar high enough in terms of being vulnerable, developing my voice, sharing my thinking, and pushing past my fears to develop to my professional potential. I realized it was time to start taking steps to become an active learner.

But learning and growing in new ways require some risk. Maybe fear holds us back or we think we aren't good enough, and those things show up when we face a challenge. Or maybe we catch ourselves comparing how we perform certain skills, how we are viewed by others, or how we worry about achieving certain outcomes.

Vulnerability isn't worrying about what others think. Instead, it's speaking from an unfiltered heart. It's having the courage to push past fear and doubt by asking for help, knowing you'll be making small gains when you consistently put yourself in learning opportunities. Try focusing your mind on the effort and not the outcome by being fully engaged in the activity in front of you. This takes the focus off trying to be perfect and, instead, allows you to enjoy the immediate challenge in front of you.

I practice vulnerability outside the classroom when I step onto a slackline, a long seatbelt-type line attached to two endpoints and varying in firmness and elasticity. Besides being vulnerable trying to walk across it, I've learned my focus shouldn't be on getting all the way across. If I only focus on reaching the end point, the slackline lets me know by bouncing me off, reminding me to focus on one step at a time. When I walk the slackline, I feel the small movements, shifting my weight from the heel onto the toe to help stay connected. Vulnerability is the ability to stay connected to your inner truth, giving up perfection, and not focusing on the outcome.

In the classroom, you may feel vulnerable when you put yourself in a situation like using new technology or new teaching strategies. You may not succeed at first, but the more you put yourself in these learning opportunities, the better you're going to become. Instead of staying stuck in the same exact spot, your initial vulnerability blossoms into a pattern of growth and strength.

Bringing It to the Classroom

Vulnerability provides an opportunity for authentic learning, and the classroom is the perfect place for students to learn vulnerability. Model lessons for students about striving for personal greatness. You're the ideal person to show them how to fail, readjust, and rise again through daily effort and grit. When students see you taking risks, they'll be more motivated to do the same, knowing you'll be there to offer empathy and positive feedback, and to encourage them to try it again using new strategies. Instead of just setting the bar for students to reach based on test scores and projected growth targets, what if we raised the bar and taught students how to deal with failure? Create an empowering classroom environment valuing vulnerability, hard work, and positivity.

Instead of just setting the bar for students to reach based on test scores and projected growth targets, what if we raised the bar and taught students how to deal with failure?

Students can also learn vulnerability from characters in books who are scared, wrong, have failed, feel rejected, or characters who, despite setbacks, are willing to put themselves in situations to tackle challenging obstacles. We can practice putting ourselves in similar situations, knowing where true learning can take place. We can come back stronger with more openness and honesty in sharing lessons and helping others.

Wholehearted characters show how vulnerability can be used as a learning springboard to achieve new heights and develop courage. As the character gains strength in her story, students can gather personal strength along with the character and embrace their own vulnerability to try more challenging activities and soar to new heights in their own lives.

We need to honor the hearts and minds of students by wholeheartedly connecting with them and challenging them. Tuck explicit mindset strategies into mini-lessons, conferences, character education lessons, and class meetings. Or use them as hooks so students can see the authentic relevance and connection in their lives. As teachers, we should be right next to our students saying, "I believe in you! You got this! Don't stop until you're proud!" Students will work with dogged determination if they know you care. It's our job to find the greatness in all our students and encourage them to reach their full potential. Don't let them settle for anything but their best.

Connect with administration, parents, and community members so everyone is invested in creating opportunities for students to take risks as we "coach in," offering one-on-one customized support with specific objectives while celebrating student effort. Collaborate with a variety of people who impact students' lives. When students see people in their community modeling big risk taking—sometimes succeeding, other times failing—students will be more apt to make bigger leaps. Collectively, we'll be the team raising the bar and celebrating the continual effort to get better.

Flex Your EduNinja Muscles

★ Finish these statements:

  ★ When things get tough, I _____

  _____ .

  ★ If I fail I _____

  _____ .

  ★ To attain success, I can try _____

  _____ .

★ In what ways are you authentically modeling failure for your students? How else might you be able to model failure for your students?

★ When do you experience perfectionism or paralysis related to trying something new? What might you say to yourself the next time those feelings come up?

★ How do you deal with a situation when it becomes difficult?

★ What do you do when you're emotionally exposed? What could you do differently the next time you feel emotionally exposed or something is difficult?

★ How are you modeling vulnerability and authenticity for your students? Are you sending the message that we're all imperfect and struggle, but are worthy of love and belonging?

An EduNinja
Overcomes Fear

6

I am always doing things I can't do.
That is how I get to do them.

—Pablo Picasso

If you had one shot, one opportunity to seize
everything you ever wanted in one moment,
would you capture it or just let it slip?

—Eminem

When my coworkers asked me what I was doing over the summer, and I told them I was speaking in front of teachers from four schools in Nebraska, I'm sure they thought this was odd. They knew I didn't raise my hand at staff meetings or talk much in larger groups, and I shied away from the spotlight. But when Dr. John Skretta, Norris superintendent, asked me to speak to his staff about incorporating foundational health and wellness strategies to enhance teaching and learning for students, I immediately said, "Yes!" As soon as I hung up the phone, I felt fear creep in. I had no speaking experience! I had a lot of work to do updating my resume and website, researching as much as possible by connecting with health and wellness organizations and watching online speakers, creating an outline and writing my speech, and creating slides.

We all have fears. The difference between our heroes and us is our heroes have the courage to look their fears in the face, grapple with them, and decide to conquer them. They make the choice to work hard every day to succeed, despite their fears. But we can do the same thing. We all have the same tools as our heroes and mentors. And we have our own opportunities to conquer our fears daily and share experiences to inspire others to do the same.

Dr. Skretta was inspiring me and helping me conquer my fears. He modestly reminded me he was mentoring me during my new learning, "leading across" by checking in, setting benchmarks, offering feedback, and encouraging me with positivity, pushing me to new levels of learning. In addition to his mentorship, I started setting up other speaking opportunities—another step toward overcoming my fear.

I was gaining courage by leading CUE professional development sessions, saying "yes" to guest podcasts, and memorizing information for vodcasts with New Teacher Center and the California Teacher's Summit. My first vodcast was absolutely terrible. In fact, I restudied, practiced, and asked to be refilmed the following day. I made new note cards, taped them to the perimeter of my computer screen, and practiced over and over. These attempts were all steps in the right direction, pushing me beyond anything I'd done in my comfort zone during my forty years prior.

Everyone is tested with fears and obstacles, which may highlight personal weakness. But instead of hiding in a safe place, an EduNinja knows that facing these fears and obstacles is what's needed to excel. Preparing for the big keynote speech wasn't an easy task, but I continued working, avoiding comparisons to others. I made this process a priority and found it was fueling my passion to create a culture of health at our school.

Fear limits our potential and leads us to make decisions that maintain safety and the status quo. We will never reach our personal greatness if we lead with fear or make decisions based on it. Fear may try to creep into our lives in many different ways, so it's important we have a plan to practice courage, rise above the fear, and lead with love in our personal and professional lives.

Overcoming the Fear of Failure

What holds you back from setting bigger goals? For me, it's usually the fear of failure. In the past, I let self-doubt or hurtful words from others stop me from setting the goals I wanted and prevent me from reaching my potential before I even tried. If you do the same, ask yourself where your limiting beliefs are originating from. Are you self-sabotaging by thinking you aren't good enough or you'll "be happy when . . ."? Or is fear coming because of someone else's words? In some instances, fear keeps us safe, but far too often fear takes hold and we sink back into security and complacency. It's time to change our mindset about fear by consistently facing it, practicing and refining tools to conquer it. For example, instead of always being comfortable and complacent, we owe it to ourselves, our families, and our students to be the best we can be by modeling and setting big, intimidating goals.

Ironically, setting *even bigger* goals and taking risks is the best way to overcoming our fear of failure. It helps us not focus on the outcome. You might think, *Wait, that doesn't make sense. If I'm already scared in the first place, why in the world would I set an even bigger goal I'm afraid to tackle?* Dreaming big makes your end goal feel like it's worth achieving. It's not that you aren't going to take steps to get to your end goal; you are. Even when you set huge goals, you'll take small steps toward them. The way we do the small things determines how we do everything. Start by tackling small fears and keep building momentum. Practice learning through failure, always knowing you're not done until you're proud. Remember it's okay to struggle, but don't give up on yourself. You're only unsuccessful when you stop trying.

Be patient. It takes time to develop skills and reach for greatness. But keeping what you truly want and *why* at the forefront will help you persevere and achieve. Don't fear the hard work or setbacks; many successful people failed multiple times before achieving success.

- Walt Disney was fired from a newspaper for lacking ideas.
- UCLA basketball coach John Wooden didn't win his first NCAA Division 1 Championship until his sixteenth season of coaching.
- Steve Jobs was initially fired from Apple.
- Oprah was told she was unfit for television.

When your purpose is stronger than your fear, you won't give up. Have radical trust and be patient with yourself in this process as you learn and grow.

Every one of us can achieve so much more than we think when we have the courage to visualize, verbalize, and put in the daily effort toward reaching our goals. Work on skills consistently, develop stamina, refine strategies, and practice a positive outlook for tackling your obstacle course. It's an exciting mindset to live by! Each day, notice what you're learning from being uncomfortable, and you're sure to find empowering lessons from pushing your limits.

Overcoming the Fear That You Aren't Good Enough

Be who you are, nothing more, nothing less.

—Michael Franti

Sometimes fear tells us we aren't good enough. We may compare ourselves to others and often feel we come up short. But you are unique and amazing in ways others are not. Love yourself—even the parts hard to love. And let people see and love you also. Courage allows our voice to take flight and boldly tell our stories. Open your heart. Be vulnerable. Be beautiful. Show the beauty of being authentic and learning to love yourself even when you are alone, hurt, not in shape, working toward your ideal career, etc.

Our goal becomes listening to our inner wisdom, making time to notice what we're feeling and not judging emotions as "good" or "bad." Our goal is to regularly take time to tune in. Don't feel pressure to feel happy all the time because this may cause you to suffer unnecessarily when emotions like fear, anger, guilt, or shame arise. Notice and feel your range of emotions. Different emotions are appropriate for different situations. Practice living wholeheartedly with courage, curiosity, and compassion.

It may be challenging at times to take an authentic look at emotions we find uncomfortable. This is where we face our fear and get to exhibit courage. When we do, we're open to opportunities to be fully alive and awake, and to experience a sense of well-being and joy. By creating time and awareness for heartfelt meditation, we learn to notice the mind-body connection and patterns associated with our feelings. We learn to relate to our joys, discomforts, and pains while consciously choosing to live with more balance, stability, and compassion. Practice heartfulness regularly. When we're aware and tuned into the moment, we can choose to live a rich, emotionally balanced, meaningful life, animated by a spirit of compassion and caring.

> *Educating the mind without educating*
> *the heart is no education at all.*
>
> —*Aristotle*

Overcoming the Fear of Not Being Ready

You may never feel ready to try something new. Maybe you catch yourself saying, "I'm not ready to run that race, but maybe the next one . . . ." Ideally, we want to get to a point where we are disciplined and consistent in our training, but let's get real: life comes first. Teaching is an exhausting job, and I don't know about you, but there are days I come home from school, fall onto the couch, and don't wake up until the next day. Despite those feelings, I always keep Coach Rose's words in my head: "You always have to be ready to go."

It's true you have to be consistently working hard if you want to pounce on an opportunity when it comes your way. But you don't have to be *perfect*. Keep your vision clear, work toward your goals, and be consistent. If you aren't ready, say "yes" and start today. Know there will be days you may need a twelve-hour nap so you can tackle the next day.

We may experience fear through the idea of perfectionism, or the willingness only to try things we know we'll finish perfectly and successfully. Face your fear and get over your self-doubt, pride, or the walls you've built up. When I'm rock climbing, I typically take routes I know I can finish instead of pushing myself to try new ones and find problems I may not be able to solve at first. I tend to only try a more difficult path when prompted by a friend. By only climbing familiar routes, I'm underestimating my abilities. To become a more dynamic and skilled climber, however, I need to try new paths and fall frequently. If you aren't making a lot of mistakes, you're likely not doing a lot of learning. Stop trying to be perfect and start pushing yourself to make more mistakes to learn and grow.

If you aren't making a lot of mistakes, you're likely not doing a lot of learning. Stop trying to be perfect and start pushing yourself to make more mistakes to learn and grow.

Overcoming the Fear of Pressure and Performance

To reach your personal greatness you need to practice under pressure. Good players can perform skills when there isn't pressure, but the *great* ones develop mental toughness by constantly putting themselves under pressure, practicing in the worst conditions, and developing strategies to achieve when the stakes are high and they're in the spotlight. Overcoming the fear of performance requires being present, using mental focus, and visualization. Before you perform, practice seeing yourself successfully completing a skill correctly. Feel every part of the action fully; feel the success. Instead of playing to lose, play to win. Avoid playing safe by playing hard, having fun in the moment and finding your passion again.

If a negative thought arises as you're performing, quickly recognize it, name it, refocus, use positive self-talk, and/or focus on your breathing. Do what you need to readjust back to the present moment. Bring awareness to your body—feel your feet on the slackline again. Staying present in sports and in life takes practice but is an amazing place to be. Rise up to pressure, be ready to shine, and crave the opportunity to perform in the moment. The focus isn't on winning. It's having an opportunity to go for it—to perform the exact skill you've repeated over and over with focus and intention. Showing mental strength and trusting yourself by giving your best, not worrying about the outcome, means you'll always be proud of your effort and passion for what you love to do.

If you're struggling, disappointed, or hitting a plateau, go back to how you used to play—with nothing to lose. If you face a setback, have faith it will lead to an opportunity for bigger growth. Never stop playing with passion. Bruce Lee said, "If you always put limits on everything you do, physical or anything else, it will spread into your work and into your life. There are no limits. There are only plateaus, and you must not stay there; you must go beyond them."

Continually look for ways to improve by pushing through your fear of pressure, practicing visualization techniques, quickly naming a negative thought and reframing it with positive thinking, and using breathing techniques to successfully get to the next level.

Overcoming the Fear of Critics and Pessimists

Your life won't come without critics and naysayers. Don't let their criticism—or praise—get into your head. Your opinion matters, not theirs. You don't need to fear the opinions from naysayers because you have taken the time to dig deep, define your core values, and purposefully align your daily actions to build your masterpiece life. So stay focused and on course. Remain motivated and strong in your convictions. Believe in your vision and your cause. When you're busy doing these things, you don't have time to worry about criticism.

Maya Angelou reminds us, "Do the best you can until you know better. Then when you know better, do better." We're all doing the best we can at this moment in time. When you believe in something bigger than yourself or your small circle, it's much easier to let criticism go.

Overcoming the Fear of "Going It Alone"

Fear of working toward success on your own can be paralyzing. In fact, we are much stronger when we are connected to other people. Phil Jackson, coach of the Chicago Bulls from 1989 to 1998, had a locker-room mantra that said, "No man is an island. No man goes his way alone. What I put into the lives of others will come back unto its own." He had one of the greatest basketball players of all time (Michael Jordan) on his team, but he still knew his players would have greater success when they worked *together*.

To overcome your fear of "going it alone," look for connections with everyone you meet. The more connected you feel toward teammates, coworkers, and mentors, the more committed to success you'll become. While striving with others for greatness, you're better able to give your daily best to achieve *personal* greatness. Being connected to other people allows you to share your joys, setbacks, and positive perspective while offering support, encouragement, and elation for breakthroughs.

Connections enable you to take what you've learned from your mentors and share that wisdom to empower others. Some days you will take the leadership role, offering support or skills training; other days you'll receive support and feel better, thanks to your team. When you wholeheartedly pursue excellence by helping others become their best, you gain a lifelong bond, one going beyond the school year or sport season. Those connections are remembered forever.

On the other hand, pride thinks you can do it alone, and it separates people and makes us artificial. Be authentic; humility is what makes us human. Everyone has something to teach us, and we can't deeply or meaningfully achieve success without the help of others. Gather, build, and strengthen your tribe. Surround yourself with people who make you hungry for life, touch your heart, and nourish your soul.

> ## Surround yourself with people who make you hungry for life, touch your heart, and nourish your soul.

Think back to all the teachers, teammates, and coaches who have helped you in the past. These heroes continue to guide you through the tough times with their perspective, support, and strength even if they aren't physically present. Picture them next to you and think of what they'd say. Be like your hero to someone within your tribe and raise the bar for your team.

Overcoming the Fear of Leadership

You're already a leader in your classroom. The next step is to become a leader *outside* your classroom. You have a wealth of talents you could share with other educators, at your school and globally, to inspire them. But you may be like I was—fearful of taking on a leadership role. Face your fear by sharing resources on social media, writing blog posts, leading workshops, or creating challenges. These are great places to start leading and learning with others. Serve and share your passion. Promote your purpose graciously and regularly to inspire others to do the same. Look at social media bios and feeds to find awesome educational leaders who are sharing innovative work in their classrooms via art, science, makerspace, and coding. We're surrounded by talented, dedicated educators. Why not collaborate? Offer your passion and fulfill your purpose as you benefit from and gain a deeper appreciation for their passion to share with you.

Overcoming the Fear of the Unknown

Facing indecision, questions, or anxiety can bring a fear of the unknown. Instead of giving in to fear, I've learned to keep at the forefront of my mind the idea of "radical trust." Radical trust is the assurance that when we make decisions based on integrity, we'll eventually get to see the reasons for the situation and how we gained important lessons from it. I've learned each situation in life moves us to another level. Recently, when faced with a fear or something unknown, I've started asking myself, "What do I really need at this moment?" Then my mind shifts and, because of radical trust, I have the opportunity to practice what I need. Cultivating radical trust means that once I notice what I need, I put myself in situations where I must learn. Growth then comes from the experience of letting go of expectations and outcomes. I don't always succeed or get the desired result but, over time, living fully in this cumulative mindful effort helps me elevate to a new level and connect the dots to meaningful learning.

Practice radical trust by looking for clues, knowing everything serves the bigger purpose of guiding you on your journey. As I've said about other things before, being present and not attaching yourself to an outcome is important. Having radical trust is a balance of actively putting in place what you need to succeed and having faith you'll be given what you need to learn and grow.

Flex Your EduNinja Muscles

★ Is fear causing you to struggle in your mind? Your body? Your spirit? How are they connected?

★ What can you do to increase your leadership role at your school and globally?

★ What are some powerful lessons you've learned that you'd like to share with others?

★ When did radical trust help you? When can radical trust help you in the future?

An EduNinja
Fuels with
Good Nutrition

*Let food be thy medicine and
medicine be thy food.*

—Hippocrates

*Even in this high-tech age, the low-tech plant continues
to be the key to nutrition and health.*

—Jack Weatherford, *Indian Givers: How the Indians
of the Americas Transformed the World*

Eating healthier has changed my life. The more I learn about healthy foods and consistently apply the strategies I gain, the more I experience improvement in mental clarity, overall wellness, and increased sustained energy, making me a better teacher who's more engaged in my lessons.

Growing up in rural Pennsylvania, I ate some very unhealthy foods. During the week, I had cereal and a cup of orange juice for breakfast. But on the weekends, breakfast included fried scrapple (a Pennsylvania Dutch mush loaf of pork scraps, combined with cornmeal and wheat or buckwheat flour), eggs, and pancakes! My lunches consisted of cream cheese wrapped in summer sausage or peanut butter and marshmallow on saltine crackers. After school, I'd have a snack of chips or pretzels, followed by a dinner of meat, potatoes, canned corn, and a glass of milk. Most nights also included a big bowl of ice cream!

These were the foods in our house, and I developed habits based on what I knew, what I was taught, and my environment. I didn't learn until I was older what foods I was supposed to be eating. Now I've become my own health advocate, empowered by asking thoughtful questions of trusted doctors, avoiding the latest diet trends, and researching what I'm putting into my body while noticing how my body responds.

I've become my own health advocate, empowered by asking thoughtful questions of trusted doctors, avoiding the latest diet trends, and researching what I'm putting into my body while noticing how my body responds.

All aspects of health and wellness are interconnected. When you listen to your body, get enough rest and exercise, and are fully tuned in to the present moment, you're able to make smarter, more disciplined decisions about what to buy at the grocery store and what to put into your body to ensure you are getting the nutrition you need for better performance, both in and out of the classroom. You might even start noticing eating patterns and potential pitfalls and be able to make a plan to get back on track.

For instance, we can get sidetracked by all the ads for tempting grocery store treats or new food items at restaurants, and we sometimes let our emotions do the choosing. It's tempting to say zucchini bread is "healthier" because it has a vegetable in it or to overlook the two to three serving-sized squeezes of agave nectar or honey you squirted into that green smoothie. And most of us have probably come home after a long school week feeling we deserve to eat whatever we want over the weekend. But these things aren't necessarily true. Being honest with yourself is the most important thing you can do to change your nutritional habits to see immediate benefits and feel better.

Triggers are another potential pitfall. We all have our favorite foods we can't say "no" to. I could easily eat a whole bag of granola in one day, even after saying I won't. Another trigger is eating traditional desserts; it's more difficult for me to stop eating sugar afterward. My solution to these triggers is to buy granola only on special occasions and eat desserts only if they're extraordinary—not every time I'm offered. Additionally, I keep healthy treats with me in case of emergencies, allowing me to better maintain balance without spinning out of sugar control.

Eating serves the purpose of fueling our bodies. My philosophy is to make healthy eating choices 90 percent of the time, and I am empowered by purposefully selecting foods to meet my nutritional needs. Fresh, natural foods fuel my body for performance and reduce my cravings. By regularly eating smaller quantities of natural foods, such as a handful of almonds, and drinking green veggie juice, I don't feel heavy and tired because less energy is being diverted to aid in digesting a bigger meal. Additionally, I don't have those huge swings in blood sugar.

The Western diet, in large part due to its high levels of sugar, sodium, and saturated fats, has contributed to chronic diseases such as heart disease, diabetes, and obesity. Choosing whole foods instead of refined foods empowers you to feel better and perform better. Read food labels at the grocery store and shop the perimeters of the store where the perishable foods are located. Small shifts in food choices, over the course of a week or a day—or even a meal—can make a big difference.

Tips to Reduce Sugars, Saturated Fats, and Sodium

Added sugars are found in yogurts, ketchup, sauces, salad dressings, soups, sports drinks, and other bottled beverages. We can't avoid it, but we can certainly reduce our intake by being mindful label readers. The American Heart Association recommends limiting the amount of added sugars we consume to six teaspoons per day for most American women and children and nine teaspoons per day for men. Many of us consume this by breakfast. By reducing the amount of added sugars we eat, we can cut calories, control weight, and potentially improve heart health.

Begin reducing your sugar intake by reading labels and avoiding items containing it in the top five ingredients. And remember, sugar has many names: corn sweetener, corn syrup, fruit juice concentrates, high-fructose corn syrup, honey, invert sugar, malt sugar, molasses, raw sugar, and molecules ending in "ose" (dextrose, fructose, glucose, lactose, maltose, sucrose). Try saving desserts for special celebrations (don't feel obligated to eat a treat on every student's birthday).

The best way to reduce the amount of saturated fats is to fill your plate with veggies. When I was young, my favorite plate was decorated with Star Wars characters and separated into sections so my food wouldn't get mixed up. Not surprisingly, I never put vegetables in the largest section of my plate. However, if I still had my plate today, I'd fill it up with vegetables. Increase your veggie intake and let foods such as sandwiches, tacos, and pizza be your side dishes. Better yet, make side dishes of whole grains or a healthier protein instead. Also, be a label reader and limit certain snacks and sweets too.

Sodium is an essential nutrient and is needed by the body in relatively small quantities unless substantial sweating occurs. Getting the sodium your body needs is easy with just a little sea salt. Eat fresh foods, only using canned or frozen foods periodically. Additionally, try to limit the amount of sandwich meat you eat.

Making It Practical

Teaching often feels like a non-stop job. As such, we may feel we're too busy or too tired to eat healthy. Grabbing food on the run can be tempting. However, as I mentioned previously, I have much more energy and mental clarity when I eat healthy foods. With a little planning, you can easily eat healthier, even during a busy school week. Try some of these planning tips on a Sunday for simplifying healthy eating during the week:

- Spiralize and cut veggies
- Prepare salad containers for lunch with greens, grains, and protein.
- Prepare oatmeal for the next few days and keep it in the fridge.
- If you eat chicken, cook or buy a rotisserie chicken and cut it up to save time.
- Cook a big batch of quinoa to eat for breakfast or lunch.
- Brew green tea on the stove and keep it in the refrigerator.
- Cut celery to eat with almond butter.

- Cut veggies to eat with hummus.
- Cut watermelon for the week or have fruit ready for snacks.

Nutrition plays a huge part in our health goals. We must be honest with ourselves, monitor the quantity and quality of foods we eat, and set short-term nutrition goals to match our overall health goals. This will ensure we're eating healthy 90 percent of the time or more and performing at our best with sustained energy in our classrooms.

Consider the following nutrition goals to focus on for a month:

- Learn and adopt the types of food and portion sizes from *ChooseMyPlate.gov.*
- Drink eight cups of water a day.
- Reduce sugar, saturated fats, and sodium.
- Eat fruits and vegetables in a variety of colors—and try new ones.
- Make a healthy foods grocery list, then stay strong and avoid tempting items by asking, "What would an EduNinja do?"
- Prepare a new healthy meal each week by cooking with family or friends.
- Pack school lunches and snacks with your kids this month, or model the healthy food you're eating at recess and lunch.
- Focus on a healthy breakfast this month.
- Go to a Farmer's Market and learn more about the foods you're eating.
- Start a school gardening program or healthy cooking lunch club.
- Bake healthier desserts and take them to a neighbor.
- Bring in healthier treats for birthday celebrations and class parties.

- Keep a food journal this month.
- Make a healthy school cookbook.

Daily Food Journal

We teachers love to share learning tools. I keep a daily food journal because it empowers me to make better choices. I notice how food plays a major part in my well-being, energy levels, and teaching performance, then rank my progress in each area:

1	seldom
2	inconsistently
3	achieving mindfully and purposefully (this is my benchmark)
4	going above and beyond

For each category I ask myself what I can put into place to improve my consistency. Sometimes purposefully planning meals or just slowing down to mindfully notice food choices, portion sizes, emotional triggers, and water consumption is all I need to stay consistent. Try keeping your own food journal. You'll be inspired to see how focusing on where you are today helps you create sustainable and simple healthy habits in the future.

Categories

Category	Rank
Food	
Water	
Sleep	

Movement	
Mindfulness/RestorativePractices	
Overall Mood	

I think of a "three" as making purposeful and mindful healthy choices. If I can mark at least a three it means that . . .

- I make healthy food choices most of the day.
- I mindfully eat smaller portions of healthy food every few hours to help prevent overeating.
- I prepare healthy meals and pack healthy food alternatives for when I'm not at home.
- I purposely eat carbs earlier in the morning and afternoon, tapering consumption later in the evening.
- I know how much sugar I am consuming daily and stay under the recommended amount.
- I eat mostly vegetables at meals, keeping other foods as side dishes.
- I get the amount of rest I need to function.
- I proactively drink water before I'm thirsty.
- If I get off track by eating an unhealthy meal, I quickly get back on track.
- I manage stress.
- I keep moving throughout the day.

Bringing It to the Classroom

When I taught my students about healthy nutrition, they were shocked to learn how much sugar was in their favorite sports drinks, school lunch choices, and snacks, compared to the amount they should be eating. Students noticed ways to reduce sugar, saturated fats, and sodium in the foods offered at school. They realized the importance of educating others about making healthier choices and loved sharing their new learning with schoolmates and families. Additionally, each student researched ways to make our school lunches healthier, wrote persuasive essays, and presented their new findings to the superintendent. As a result, a school wellness committee will be formed and a potential action plan put into place for making school lunches healthier. Students at our school have also become lunch club gardeners. They love seeing firsthand how to plant, care for, grow, and consume healthy veggies—from dinosaur kale and sugar snap peas to green onions. Eating more vegetables has become a lifestyle to them.

As teachers, we are leaders with a lot of people watching us. We have an awesome opportunity to make a positive impact on the healthy eating habits of those who look to us for strategies and knowledge. We must lead by example, taking care of ourselves first. Then we can share our new learning to inspire healthy habits for students, families, and our school community of teachers and staff. We can start by sharing these basic nutrition principles—a few simple changes suggested by the American Heart Association:

Limit	sugary drinks, sweets, fatty meats, and salty or highly processed foods
Avoid	partially hydrogenated oils, tropical oils, and excessive calories
Replace	highly processed foods with homemade or less-processed options
Enjoy	a variety of nutritious foods from all the food groups, especially fruits & veggies
Keep	healthy habits even when you eat away from home

> **As teachers, we are leaders with a lot of people watching us. We have an awesome opportunity to make a positive impact on the healthy eating habits of those who look to us for strategies and knowledge.**

I am passionate about healthy eating! Visit my website at *eduninja.net* if you're interested in learning more specific ways to make healthy food choices, try new recipes, or if you have more questions. I have lots of information to share about behaviors that support healthy eating habits!

Flex Your EduNinja Muscles

★ Ask yourself, "Why do I want to eat healthy?" and hold that idea front and center when you select foods to eat.

★ What food non-truths do you tell yourself? How can you combat those non-truths?

★ What are your food triggers? How can you combat those triggers?

★ What food habits would you like to change? What new food habits would you like to implement?

★ How can you reduce sugar, saturated fats, and sodium consumption throughout your day?

★ How can you help students reduce sugar, saturated fats, and sodium consumption throughout their day?

★ What are some realistic healthy food alternatives for you?

An EduNinja
Moves

> For physical fitness is not only one of the most important keys to a healthy body; it is the basis of dynamic and creative intellectual activity. The relationship between the soundness of the body and the activities of the mind is subtle and complex. Much is not yet understood. But we do know what the Greeks knew: that intelligence and skill can only function at the peak of their capacity when the body is healthy and strong, that hardy spirits and tough minds usually inhabit sound bodies.

> —John F. Kennedy

Summers can be a great time for teachers to start, peak, or stay on top of their fitness game. We feel like pros during the summers—waking up refreshed and without an alarm, fully enjoying our morning tea or coffee. We read for pleasure, enjoy our workouts with friends, and make fresh foods for every meal. Summertime is a teacher's dream for getting sixty minutes of movement a day—at the beach, in the mountains, or on the lake!

How do we take this stress-free vibe and positive attitude into our school year workouts? Starting the school year doesn't have to be the end of our summer gains in the gym. By adopting the EduNinja

Mindset, we give ourselves the gift of moving throughout our entire school day by planning our daily, monthly, and yearly movements to ensure we're building healthy habits and staying on top of our teaching game.

The EduNinja Mindset is the authentic mindset we have to have, committing on the very first day of school and maintaining momentum. This year was my twentieth year of teaching—and by far my best. I'm definitely not ready to retire yet, because this coming year is going to be even better! (Sorry last year's class, but that's the EduNinja Mindset kicking in again!) My best years of teaching have been the ones when I've been the healthiest, and since I'm still refining and improving my health and wellness knowledge, I know I'll be even happier and making healthier choices in future years!

As educators, we get to be health advocates for teachers and students by modeling lifelong health, nutrition, wellness, and fitness for children, families, and our global community. We have the awesome opportunity to give students lifelong tools to live healthy lives. We get to give them the gift of wellness. Maybe they'll be inspired to become a health advocate for their school or make significant world changes one day.

Associate Clinical Professor of Psychiatry, Harvard Medical School, John Ratey, MD, believes, "Exercise is the single best thing you can do for your brain in terms of mood, memory, and learning."

To inspire wellness and fitness, we have to adopt it and model it. In this chapter, I'm going to share numerous ideas to help you add movement to your personal life and in your classroom. You may be thinking:

- That sounds great, but where will I find the time?
- Adding movement to my classroom sounds fun, but how will I have the stamina to lead these activities?
- How can I make it work in my classroom when I have X-number of students and zero funding?
- What if I have students who don't want to move?
- What if my principal doesn't believe in this work?

All of those thoughts are opportunities for the EduNinja Mindset to explore and create ways for you to "ninja" and find the answers. Improving your own fitness and adding kinesthetic learning to support your students is important. Starting small is the key.

Take the time to build rapport with your administration and, eventually, get their support to help lead a healthier, more active classroom of learners. If you are determined and willing to inspire healthy teachers and students while meeting the needs of all learners, including the kinesthetic ones, you will find a way to do it. Once you get administrator approval, be sure to involve parents too.

Movement Starts with You

Workouts don't have to be sixty minutes long. Our fourth grade math standards remind us there are multiple ways to divide the number sixty. Movement breaks, teacher lunch workouts, or solo workouts can happen in three twenty-minute sessions, two thirty-minute sessions, or sessions of twenty and forty minutes. Find a schedule you can work with and be consistent!

There are also a variety of times throughout the day you can work out. You may be an "early bird" who chooses to go to bed an hour earlier, wake up an hour earlier, and get your day started with a morning workout. Personally, I don't understand people who like working out in the morning. I'm "frenemies" with the idea. I hate it unless by "morning" you mean 10:30 a.m. Then I love it! How many times have you heard people say, "I've tried working out before school, but it's just not me." Obviously, I've had similar thoughts. When we feel this way, we have to ask ourselves, "What one thing gets us to the gym even when we don't want to go?" A bigger health or performance goal or meeting friends for mutual motivation is often the answer. If you still can't get out of bed, it may be time to set a bigger goal.

There are actually several benefits to working out in the morning, the first being we have less chance of putting it off or, worse, never getting around to it at all. Working out in the morning also increases metabolism, burning more calories throughout the day, and improves mood by releasing endorphins. The endorphin release is the feeling we all love after a workout. Personally, I feel exponentially energized and better prepared to teach students after a morning workout.

Whether you're practicing yoga, walking with friends, or heading out the door for your morning run, your workout is time you've created for yourself. Commit to this because it's truly a gift you give yourself. And everyone around you benefits as well from your increased energy, positive mood, and enhanced focus.

Morning workouts also create more time after school for other priorities. When something "comes up" after school—or you're like me and are usually ready for a nap then—you won't miss your workout. By working out in the morning, you'll also avoid the nagging guilt of pretending you're going to make an after-dinner workout. Instead, do what I've learned helps keep me at my best: pack your gym and food bags the night before, wake up consistently, and work out in the morning.

Commit to working out two to three mornings a week. Even if you only have time for a twenty-minute workout at home, you'll see results if you're consistent and your diet and hydration are on point.

Take Sunday night to plan your daily workouts the way you plan your lesson plans.

Movement Breaks Throughout the Day

Smaller workouts sprinkled throughout the day may be easier to commit to. School recess is an opportunity to move; I see teachers walking the stairs at our school every day. Lunchtime is another great opportunity to get moving again. You might think working through lunch is a way to leave early, but I've found it's like trying to hold sand in your hands. If you work through your lunch break, you push your brain beyond the break time you need and quickly ingest your food, all without getting any quality work done. When the bell rings for the students to return after lunch, you're left feeling tired and usually unaccomplished. Teachers are known for working endlessly, oftentimes at the expense of their own well-being. Try doing your work *after* you take a movement break.

According to the American Heart Association, "A healthy school environment can result in greater academic achievement and healthier students and school staff." Some teachers on our campus have taken a proactive approach by modeling healthy habits on campus. Teachers are saying *yes* to fitness and wellness throughout the day by

According to the American Heart Association, "A healthy school environment can result in greater academic achievement and healthier students and school staff."

committing to workouts before school, taking brain breaks with students, and participating in lunch clubs. School lunch clubs are a great way for teachers to lead, connect, and inspire students or coworkers to keep moving to meet the daily goal of sixty minutes of physical activity.

EduNinja™ Fit

I started EduNinja™ Fit at our school, and these are my favorite three days of the week. I look forward to seeing teachers and students for thirty minutes of core exercises, bodyweight exercises, Swiss Ball exercises, or yoga. The purpose of the EduNinja™ Fit is to inspire lifelong health and wellness strategies. While I would highly recommend you start a similar program, please get the proper training and certification from an accredited organization and please consult your administration before implementing any exercise practice for teachers or students on campus.

EduNinja™ Fit participants start with eating a healthy lunch, learning how to make informed food choices, and experiencing the benefits of sound nutrition. After being properly fueled, we practice strength, balance, speed, agility, and flexibility in this fun fitness class. We start the trimester by learning the basic principles of yoga and mindfulness, then transition to simple bodyweight exercises, and end the trimester with playground obstacle course work.

Visit eduninja.net to learn what a PUMPkin workout is, what partner workouts look like, or what fun new exercises you can add each month to stay motivated and engaged in your learning.

September	Yoga, Swiss Ball, and Core Workouts
October	Yoga and PUMPkin Workouts
November	Partner Workouts
December	Partner Workouts
January	#EduNinja30 Challenge
February	Bodyweight Stations
March	Bodyweight and Exercise Prop Stations
April	Playground Workouts
May	Playground Workouts
June	Field Day Training

As the year progresses, we add small props, such as Swiss Balls, pumpkins, light backpacks, and reams of paper as our strength, stamina, and knowledge increase. At the end of the year, activities shift to the playground and we build upon our training by promoting the value of teamwork.

Teachers on our campus have been so grateful for the opportunity to work out together, and I love being able to share my passion with my friends.

I loved working out with like-minded people who care about overall health and fitness so much they are willing and ready to meet before school. I loved learning new moves and being coached and encouraged by the best EduNinja I know! Starting my day with these workouts made me feel empowered and energized. I felt stronger as the weeks went on, and I loved the way my clothes were fitting. And I didn't need caffeine to get me jump started!

—Tanya Baumgardner, middle school
science teacher

The EduNinja workouts have provided the physical benefits you would expect from exercising with a pro. But the biggest benefit I have gained from being part of this group is the reminder we teachers need to take care of ourselves. It is hard to take time out of my busy teaching day to exercise, but when I do, I always go back to my classroom refreshed and more ready to teach.

—Danika Severino, MEd, language arts teacher

For any who might want to use school dress codes as an excuse to not work out, it's easy to layer your workout clothes or change into them. Depending on the sweat meter for the workout, I mix it up. We can usually get through a core workout wearing regular school clothes, but we might need to change for other workouts. Many days I wear street style, loose-fit workout pants in black "sport material," since they can pass for dress pants yet still move well. I pair those with a loose tank top to work out in and cover my arms with a light cardigan sweater for the classroom. I also wear sportier shoes since I move with the kids all day.

Sometimes we just need time to revitalize and reenergize during lunch; that's why I teach yoga during EduNinja™ Fit. It's a great way to finish the week while focusing on building community and practicing mindfulness strategies, which are also transferable to the classroom.

The most important message is that healthier teachers make better role models who inspire students to value lifelong healthy habits as the foundation to success. Students want to rise up to elevated health challenges when they see their teacher modeling health and wellness strategies and explicitly teaching them in integrated lessons to students. Teachers and students are more engaged in learning when they are healthy, supported, and challenged. Get out of your classroom and try leading a core workout yoga class, running club or fitness lunch club with your credentialed P.E. teacher. You'll feel better and help others feel better too.

Bringing It to the Classroom

As a teacher, let your EduNinja mindset shine. Get creative with your grade level standards, your curriculum lessons, cross-curricular activities, and your physical environment. Think about the amazing opportunities for movement-based learning during field trips, plays, the arts, or virtual field trips. Consider partnering with other classrooms and other schools when creating kinesthetic lessons for your students. And don't assume kinesthetic learning has to stop at school. What about assigning kinesthetic learning homework to help with classroom concepts? Why not add in monthly fitness challenges?

The options for adding movement into your classroom are endless. You will likely find your students will be more engaged and focused, and your students *and you* will have fun in the process! Two of my favorite ways to incorporate movement are through Brain Breaks and adding kinesthetic lessons to my curriculum.

Brain Breaks in the Classroom

According to John J. Ratey, MD, associate clinical professor of psychiatry at Harvard Medical School, "Your brain can only focus for ninety to one-hundred twenty minutes before it needs a break ... A brain break every ninety minutes means taking five minutes to break the cycle of thought or action you're in to unplug from the activity."

While I'm writing this book, I'm peering at the pull-up bar out of the corner of my eye; it's begging me to practice the art of taking regular activity breaks to do my best thinking and work. But what exactly are brain or activity breaks and how do they help us in the classroom?

Brain breaks are short bursts of physical and mental exercises that help rewire the brain for higher learning, a sense of calm focus, and better mood. In the classroom it may be a five-minute group exercise or mindfulness activity. Outside the classroom, it may be a ten-minute recess activity on the playground structure, a lunchtime basketball game, or learning a new dance in P.E. I love that invigorating, heart-pumping feeling of being alive, noticing my breath, and refocusing after doing EduNinja™ Fit exercises on the playground.

"Activity helps the brain in so many ways," said James F. Sallis, a professor of family medicine and public health at the University of California, San Diego, who has done research on the association between activity breaks and classroom behavior. "Activity stimulates more blood vessels in the brain to support more brain cells. And there is evidence that active kids do better on standardized tests and pay attention more in school."

The key is to keep moving throughout the day. Our class takes two daily movement breaks in the classroom, one morning recess break, a lunch recess, and physical education class two times a week.

Dr. John Ratey boasts of the benefits of exercise and improved brain performance. He describes how brain chemicals released during exercise, including serotonin and dopamine, help create an alert brain, ready to learn. Many researchers believe exercise is beneficial in moderating hormonal fluctuations, ADHD, stress, anxiety

According to the American Heart Association, students perform better academically, have better attendance, and behave better in class after physical activity.

and mood, and in improving academic achievement. Additionally, according to the American Heart Association, students perform better academically, have better attendance, and behave better in class after physical activity.

I've seen these benefits in my students who are moving and learning, and you will too. Below are lots of brain break activities to help you get started. Try a few—or try them all. It's time to get moving with your students!

Just reminder to consult your administrator, involve your credentialed P.E. teacher, and to get certified by a reputable organization to ensure proper form of exercises and the safety of students. Students in our class love these movement breaks so it's important for students to be more than an arm's length apart from one another and at least a full body's length to enjoy these fun movements.

Guided Stretches Or Yoga Poses

Lead your students in stretches or poses, focusing on proper form and breath. Simple balancing poses work well, such as mountain pose, tree, eagle, hand-to-knee, crow, airplane or warrior three. Only do these if you know the proper form. If not, please go to eduninja.net.

Speed Skaters

Try leading a quick burst of speed skaters by bounding laterally, touching opposite arm to opposite foot. For example, first bound right, touching left hand toward right toe and keeping your gaze forward. Then bound left, reaching your right hand toward left toe and repeat. Set a timer and encourage students to continue for thirty seconds to a minute. Let them rest and then repeat.

Move Like an Animal

Call out the name of an animal, telling students to move the way the animal would. After a few seconds, call out the name of another animal and repeat for as long as desired. Bears, crabs, snakes, monkeys, frogs, and birds are animals students especially enjoy imitating.

Partner Leg Workout

Students pair up and face their partners to mirror each movement. Students perform each movement for forty-five seconds. Movements can include:

- Regular squats: Partners can hold hands as they squat.
- Sumo squats: Students do a regular squat, but on their ascent, they lift their left knee to meet their left elbow in a side crunch. On the next squat, they alternate to the right.

Musical Chairs

Organize small groups of musical chairs games.

The "Wave"

Lead students in a "wave" like you would do at a football game.

Around the World Lunges

Starting with their right leg, students lunge forward, to the right, and then to the back. They switch to their left foot and lunge back, to the left, and then forward. Repeat for one to two minutes. The front knee should not extend beyond the toes of the front foot. The back knee should go straight down toward the floor but not touch.

Sports Action

Call out a sport and a specific action from the sport for the students to emulate. Take a moment to correctly model the skill or have a coach come into class. For example: volleyball (serve a jump serve, dig a ball, block a ball, spike a ball, set a ball); or basketball (shoot a jump shot, jump to rebound, pass the ball, cross dribble, block a shot, jump for a jump ball, make a defensive move to the left and right, or dunk a basketball); or baseball (hit a ball, field a ground ball and throw it to first, pitch a fastball, catch a pop fly and throw it to the cut-off man, be the catcher and throw it to the second baseman).

Partner Bodyweight Exercises

Model exercises like paddy cake push-ups, paddy cake partner sit-ups with interlocked ankles, around the world core partner leg circles, partner core leg throw downs, bicep and tricep partner resistance. Go to my website, eduninja.net, or any reputable source to see these modeled.

Silent Ball

Students sit on the desktop and toss a Koosh ball to each other. A student is "out" if they talk, miss a catch, or throw an uncatchable throw.

Station Rotation

Create four different stations (jumping jacks, mountain climbers, sit-ups, push-ups, etc.). Model and coach students in the proper form of each station activity. Divide students into four groups. Each group performs one of the activities for forty-five seconds and then the groups rotate within fifteen seconds to the next station. Continue until all students have been to each station.

Follow the Leader

Can you head out to recess a few minutes early playing follow the leader? Students stay in a line to the playground and continue playing on the playground equipment in this follow-the-leader line.

Jumping Series

Pretend to jump rope, do jump lunges and jumping jacks.

Mirror Drill

Partners face one another and hold their palms up in front of their chests. The leader will move one hand at a time, and the follower will mirror the movement. Switch after one minute.

Backpack Workout

Use a light weighted backpack for squats, front shoulder raises, and bicep curls.

Squats

Stand with your feet shoulder-width apart. Bend your knees and lower yourself down (like you are sitting into a chair) to a ninety-degree angle, making sure you can see your toes the whole time. Then stand back up.

Front Shoulder Raises

Use a light backpack for this exercise. Start standing straight with your arms facing down, holding the backpack straight against your thighs. Keeping your arms straight and without swinging them, slowly lift the light backpack up to the front with only a slight bend on the elbow and the palms of the hands always facing down. Continue to go up until your arms are slightly above parallel to the floor. Pause then slowly lower.

Bicep Curl

Grab both straps of the backpack (palms facing upwards). Keep your elbows pressed tight to your sides, then slowly bring the backpack in toward your chest and lower down toward the starting position.

Victory Dance

Students pretend to run up the *American Ninja Warrior* "warped wall," hit the red button, and do a top-of-the-warped-wall-red-button-hitting dance; students pretend to catch a football, run into the end zone, and do a touchdown dance.

Mindful Breathing

Students stand up and put one hand on their heart and the other on their stomachs as they close their eyes and focus on breathing in and out for five full breaths. Have them notice how they feel before they sit down.

Plank Series

- *High Plank*: Lie face down in a push-up position. Keep your hands firmly pressed onto the floor and pressed in tight next to your shoulders. Keep your feet flexed and toes on the floor. Press up into a push-up. Your entire body should be in a straight line from head to core to toes. Draw your navel toward your spine and squeeze your buttocks. Keep your gaze at the floor slightly in front of you. Hold for at least ten seconds and lower back to the floor.
- *Low Plank*: Lie face down with your forearms on the floor and your elbows directly beneath your shoulders. Keep your feet flexed with your toes on the floor. Clasp your hands in front of your face as you press up to your toes; only your forearms and toes will touch the floor. Your entire body should be in a straight line from head to core to toes. Draw your navel toward your spine and squeeze your buttocks. Keep your gaze at the floor slightly in front of you. Hold for at least ten seconds and lower back to the floor.

Jumping

Model some fun jumping with forty-five seconds of ski jumps and forty-five seconds of star jumps.

Tape Balancing

Split the class into thirds. Put three long pieces of blue painting tape on the ground. Have students balance on a piece of tape, one behind the other.

Muscle Flex

Practice flexing your muscles by teaching students the muscle names and giving them a squeeze when you call them out. Have students focus on the sensation and remember the names to use when they practice other exercises.

Tricep Dips

Start by sitting in your chair. Put hands on the seat of the chair, almost sitting on them, keeping elbows in tight. Walk legs out straight or bend ninety degrees. Bend elbows slightly, keeping them in tight to your midline as you lower your body and down. Be mindful not to lock out your elbows.

Wall Sits

Instruct students to sit against the wall with feet shoulder width apart (with their bottoms off the ground) and make sure their knees and buttocks do not go below ninety degrees. Students should be able to see their own toes. Pass a ball or a light backpack up and down the line of students.

Popsicle Stick Workout

Write different exercises on popsicle sticks, then pull and complete for thirty seconds each. Example: push-ups, sit-ups, Russian twists, side planks, squats, lunges, star jumpers, etc.

Alphabet Core Workout

This section could be used by picking one core exercise per letter per day during P.E., as brain breaks or as a monthly challenge. Please go to eduninja.net for videos.

Lead students in thirty-second bursts of exercises beginning with letters of the alphabet. Please go to eduninja.net for full explanations and to see the library of photos and video clips.

A	Almonds
B	Burpees, Boat Pose, Bird Dogs
C	Crunches, Cross Body Crunches, Cat and Cow Poses, Cobra
D	Downward Dog, Double Knee Squeeze Bicycles
E	Eraser Pass Between the Legs, Elevators
F	Flutter Kicks, Frog Sit-up, Forearm Plank
G	Get-ups from Knees
H	Hollow Hold, Hollow Rocks, Hundreds, Hip Raise
I	Inchworms, Inside-out Almonds
J	Jumping Jacks, Plank Jumps, Mogul Ski Jumps
K	Knee-ins, Knee Reaches
L	Leg Raises, Lateral Plank Walk
M	Mountain Climbers, Mountain Climber Twist
N	Narrow Hands Push-ups
O	Oblique Crunches, Opposite Hand to Opposite Toe
P	Plank, Plank Shoulder Taps, Plank Jacks, Plank with Rotation, Planks with Opposite Elbow to Opposite Knee, Penguins (toe taps), Pulse-ups, Push-ups with Leg to the Side
Q	Quick Bicycles, Quick Feet

R	Rope Climbers, Russian Twists, Reverse Crunches
S	Snow Angels, Supermans, Swimmers, Side Planks, Scissor Kicks, Scissor Switch, Spiderman Planks, Slow Motion Bicycles, Side Bends, Sumo Squats
T	T-ins
U	Up Down Planks
V	V-Ups
W	Windshield Wipers, Warrior Three Balance Movements
X	Xs and Os
Y	Y-raise from Superman
Z	Zen Pose or Zig Zag Hops

Moving Beyond Brain Breaks

In my class, we're constantly moving and connecting with kinesthetic lessons. My students know having an EduNinja as a teacher means they're in for major goal setting, lots of trying, failing, repeating, refining goals, celebrating learning, participating in monthly physical challenges, daily movement breaks, mindfulness activities, lunch clubs, and building community by meeting outside of school for field trips where we learn together.

Because we move throughout the day, movement isn't a distraction; instead, movement breaks enhance learning. I've discovered if my lessons of direct instruction are strong but compact (under ten minutes), students are able to focus better, especially after a movement break. With so much movement, you may get the impression our class is loud, chaotic, or disruptive. But it isn't. In fact, our superintendent has walked in multiple times, probably expecting a highly energized environment. However, he often finds a class so quiet he doesn't realize anyone is in the classroom until he turns the corner to see engaged students on Swiss balls working quietly.

In addition to movement breaks, some students benefit by instruction involving movement. Many are tactile learners who learn best by "moving" and "doing." Some teachers who may not be as sensitive to different types of learners may assess a highly kinesthetic learner as a distraction or a behavior problem. But those are the students I *want* in my class—the active or sports-centered children or the ones who love to build and create. Those are the students I'm especially mindful of because of my own experience as a kinesthetic learner. These students especially enjoy lessons with movement because they may have spent their prior years sitting in a more sedentary classroom.

Because so many students benefit from the combination of visual, auditory, and kinesthetic learning, kinesthetic lessons can help all students learn better. Movement engages teachers and students, and kinesthetic learning lets your kids *feel* and *experience* science, math, and language arts lessons. Kinesthetic lessons can be done as a whole class or in small groups and can be done by students in pairs or independently.

Look at your current lessons and ask how you could make them more movement based. Could an activity or lesson be taught somewhere else on campus with more space to allow for movement? Could a homework assignment be turned into a kinesthetic activity? Think about learners who like hands-on science experiments, field trips where students get to make or create things, or social studies and language arts role-playing opportunities in the classroom. Keep these students in mind when you are creating your lessons.

If you're not sure who your tactile learners are, consider using an assessment to determine this. I have students take a quick assessment to see what learning style is highly developed. This gives me information, but it's also important for students to know their own prominent learning style so they can use strategies aligned for success. For example, the kinesthetic kid might make flash cards, build models, or design a project.

Adding Movement to Your Lessons

If you're still new to movement-based teaching, start where it seems the most manageable for you. Below, I've shared a couple of examples to show how a traditional lesson can be modified to better meet the needs of kinesthetic learners in a fun, engaging way. If you have questions or need more ideas, please email me, go to my website (eduninja.net), or connect on social media. I'd love to help out.

Math Multiple Towers

Adding movement to a fourth grade lesson about factors and multiples practice is easy. Kindergarten through third grade teachers can easily adapt some of these ideas to addition and subtraction facts practice as well.

Goal

Students will be able to determine the difference between a factor and a multiple, find factor pairs, and consistently and accurately know multiplication facts.

Setup and Materials

This activity is designed for four groups of six students in eight- to ten-minute stations. Materials needed include an agility ladder (or tape one on the floor), two sets of red, orange, yellow, green, and purple yarn cut into lengths of six, ten, fourteen, eighteen, and twenty-two inches respectively, two individual white boards, three firm Nerf-like balls (about the size of an adult's head) that can be dribbled with little noise, three small Koosh balls, and printouts of the multiplication facts and direction cards for stations.

Lesson

Introduce vocabulary terms: factor, factor pair, prime, composite, multiple. Teach your lesson with guided and independent practice. If there are students who need an additional reteaching opportunity, reteach in one of your stations.

Small Group with Teacher or Independent Work

Students will make eleven different "multiplication fact towers" for their number two through number twelve math facts. Check for accuracy so they can use this tool at the kinesthetic stations. Multiple towers are vertical boxes students fill in with multiplication facts and answers. For example, a "two's tower" starts at the base with "2 x 1 = 2" up to "2 x 12 = 24" at the top of the tower. Students will make eleven towers and check for accuracy. You can use a blank template of boxes or towers or have students draw their own.

Kinesthetic Stations

- Multiple Tower Agility Ladder
- Materials needed: Agility ladder and a copy of multiplication facts or multiple towers.
- Directions: The student leader in each small group reads the number or "multiplication tower" they would like their group to say. Students say the products in order as each student hops through the agility ladder. It's the job of the leader to check for accuracy. Rotate so everyone gets a chance to be the leader.

- Partner Yarn Factor Rainbows
- Materials needed: Thirty number cards with a number on the front and the factor pairs on the back and six white boards.
- Directions: Each pair of students picks a number card (for example, 8) and lists all the factor pairs in order (1, 2, 4, 8) at the bottom of an individual whiteboard. Then the students create a yarn rainbow connecting the factor pairs. Flip the card over to be sure all the factor pairs are included in your rainbow.
- Partner Multiple Dribble
- Materials needed: Three Nerf-like balls that bounce
- Directions: The leader uses the multiple tower to call out a number. The other partner dribbles and says the multiples. It's the leader's job to check for accuracy. Alternate between partner and leader.
- Factor Pair Koosh Ball Throw
- Materials needed: Three Koosh Balls and three copies of multiplication facts or multiple towers.
- Directions: In a partnership or small group, a student picks a number card. Students toss the Koosh ball back and forth as the partnership says the factor pairs for the number in order. Together they check the back of the card for accuracy.

Spelling Movement Stations

Goal

Students will be able to recognize prefixes in words to decipher word meaning and then spell words correctly (or whatever your spelling lesson goal may be). You could easily differentiate this lesson for students by using different word lists with each group.

Setup and Materials

Post on an overhead projector or share online with students a fif-teen-word list with the prefixes un-, re-, mis, dis- and the defini-tions. Have the prefix meanings and definitions covered.

Lesson

Students will be introduced to prefixes un-, which means "not"; re-, which means "again" or "back"; mis-, which means "bad" or "badly"; and dis-, which means "not" or "undo."

Step 1: Have students notice words with the same prefix and what they have in common to reasonably guess what the prefix may mean. Do this by having them turn and talk to a partner then having them share with the whole class.

Step 2: Uncover the prefix meanings and have students turn their notebooks horizontally to write the prefixes and meanings in their notebooks. (Keeping the word defini-tions covered.)

Step 3: Have students create and title four columns on their papers. Column one is titled "word" and is where they write the word. Column two is titled "educated guess" and is where they write what they believe the word means. Column three is titled "definition," and column four is titled "picture."

Step 4: Have students fill out columns one and two.

Step 5: Uncover the definitions on your shared word list and have students reexamine their lists to see how their edu-cated guess compares.

Step 6: Have students write the actual definition in column three and draw a quick sketch in column four.

Small Group with Teacher or Independent Work

Students are divided into four spelling groups. Tuesday through Thursday, each group goes to a different station to practice spelling for fifteen minutes. Two of these are kinesthetic stations.

Station 1: I lead one inquiry-based spelling lesson group to introduce word patterns, questions, and noticings. I also model a new kinesthetic spelling activity and expectations with the group.

Station 2: Online spelling app station.

Station 3: Kinesthetic spelling activity.

Station 4: Kinesthetic spelling activity.

Within each kinesthetic spelling group, students partner up so one partner can do the activity while the other carefully checks the spelling word list. Students then switch places. Some students may prefer to work independently at times. Just have them check the spelling word list before and after each word is spelled. Your specific stations will depend on the number of students and supplies you have. For example, at my spelling sandbox station, I have two sandboxes for two pairs of students.

While there are many options for kinesthetic spelling stations, here are a few of my favorites:

- Write spelling words in a sand-filled pencil box.
- Spell words while dribbling a ball.
- Spell words while moving through an agility ladder.
- Partner Koosh Ball throw: Each student spells a letter of the word while throwing the Koosh Ball to her partner. When

the word has been spelled, students collectively check the list to ensure it's correct.

- Wall Ball Spell: Students spell words while bouncing a firm Nerf ball against the wall.
- Students write their spelling words using a stylus and the colorful Paper by FiftyThree app on an iPad.
- Students act out and spell the words using Educreations for comic strips, commercials, or stories.
- Spelling Balancing Stations: On a balance disc, students practice balancing on one leg while spelling words, alternating legs every word or in a timed segment.

EduNinja Movement Homework

Exercise and movement don't stop when the school day ends. After school there are plenty of fitness activities for the whole family to enjoy. Encourage your students and their families to try a new activity together like yoga, martial arts, rock climbing, or training for an upcoming event. As the EduNinja, I actually give my students and their families homework to do together. Students (and their families) know, from the time they get their August letter informing them they are in my class, that the year will involve fun kinesthetic homework and action-based weekend field trips.

Encourage your students and their families to try a new activity together like yoga, martial arts, rock climbing, or training for an upcoming event.

Each month I give my students and their families a movement challenge and a nutrition focus to practice together. While the challenge is optional, of course, I love when students empower their families to eat better and move more. In the United States, one-third of children and nearly two-thirds of adults are obese, according to the American Heart Association. These kinds of challenges to our students can help us take one step at a time to make positive changes in our students' health.

Start building your classroom movement with monthly challenges as well. For example, in September, we start our sit-up challenge on the first day of September with one sit-up. On the second, we do two sit-ups, and so on. These challenges can be completed as brain breaks (with administrator approval), or they can be completed at recess or home. As you get toward the end of the month, you can easily break up the sit-ups—for example, three sets of ten sit-ups on the thirtieth of September. Find whatever combination works for you and visit my website (eduninja.net) to see the correct form and to get specific exercise ideas.

EduNinja Monthly Challenges

As a class, keep your daily EduNinja Monthly Challenge goal up on the board so it's visible. At the beginning of each day, write your daily goal and then erase it when you meet it, or erase and rewrite it as you get closer to meeting it throughout the day. Students may want to keep an individual running tally of meeting these goals at home and at school. You may also want to keep a class count of how many exercises the class can do as a group. These numbers might even carry over into your math block for some authentic word problems and problem-solving.

September	Sit-up Challenge
October	Push-up Challenge
November	Running Challenge
December	Squat Challenge
January	#EduNinja30 Challenge
February	Yoga Challenge
March	Jump Rope Challenge
April	Jumping Jacks
May	Burpee Challenge
June	Field Day Practice

Flex Your EduNinja Muscles

★ What obstacles get in your way when starting monthly physical challenges?

★ What obstacles prevent you from sustaining monthly physical challenges?

★ How could you encourage other classes or your whole school to complete the EduNinja Monthly Challenges together?

★ What could you do to encourage your Professional Learning Network on social media to complete the EduNinja Monthly Challenges?

★ What other community members might want to get involved? How?

An EduNinja
Practices Mindfulness

The most beautiful things in the world cannot be seen or even touched; they must be felt with the heart.

—Helen Keller

As I wrote this section, I was anxious. My publishing deadline was less than a week away, and the first day of school was quickly approaching. I had a constricted feeling in my chest, I was uncomfortable, and I'd only starting my writing for the night, already wondering how much I could possibly accomplish before the coffee shop closed. I'd just had an almond milk latte, trying to help the process, but I could only hope my writing brain would cooperate.

My mind was in the future, not connected to the present moment. On the outside I appeared calm, but inside my thoughts were racing. I was unfocused and feeling doubtful about accomplishing quality work. I was not in the ideal state of mind to be writing a chapter on *mindfulness.* Ironic.

The good news is, I noticed how I was feeling, and noticing is the first step to being mindful.

I stopped typing, inhaled slowly through my nose, and exhaled slowly through my mouth. I focused on my breath, making it fill my chest even bigger and then pushing out every last bit of breath. I purposefully took slower and bigger breaths. If my attention went to my computer screen or another thought entered my head, I refocused on my breathing.

I continued my "mindful breathing" for a couple of minutes. No one noticed. The music in the coffee shop played on and the conversations continued—all while my thoughts slowed down, and I felt the chatter in my brain dissipate. I was much calmer and no longer heard the background noise of doubt. The mindful breathing allowed me to lower my heart rate and envision the opening paragraph of this chapter. My external world didn't change, but by applying mindful breathing, I was able to attain peace of mind for a sustained amount of time and then reapply mindful breathing as I needed.

What Is Mindfulness?

If you ask five people what mindfulness is, you may get five different answers. As such, when defining *mindfulness*, it's important to look to the wisdom of those who have been practicing and teaching mindfulness strategies for years. Jon Kabat-Zinn, PhD and professor of medicine emeritus at the University of Massachusetts Medical School, established the world-renowned Mindfulness-Based Stress Reduction Clinic in 1979 and helped bring mindfulness to the mainstream. Jon Kabat-Zinn's clinical research focused on mind-body connections and strategies to help individuals suffering from stress and chronic pain. He defines mindfulness as "the awareness that arises through paying attention on purpose, in the present moment, nonjudgmentally, in the service of self-understanding and wisdom." Mindfulness is understanding our mind and noticing our present experience with clarity by using all of our senses without attached judgment.

Mindfulness is a way to keep our brains healthy, support self-regulation, and aid in effective decision-making to protect ourselves from toxic stress. In intense situations, our fight-or-flight response kicks in instinctively because our brain activates neural pathways of fear. But these same neural pathways can be activated by chronic stress due to prolonged day-to-day worries, ruminating about a negative event, or replaying repeated feelings of guilt. The more these high-stress-response fear pathways are activated, the more they become our default setting.

Mindfulness is a way to keep our brains healthy, support self-regulation, and aid in effective decision-making to protect ourselves from toxic stress.

The good news is we have the power to change this simply by changing our focus. Neuroplasticity is the idea that the brain is always changing; therefore, we can create new positive patterns of thinking. With repetition, new positive thinking connections are strengthened while old stressful thought patterns become less prominent. We can change the structure and function of our brains to become more stress resilient. According to UCLA psychiatry professor Dr. Dan Siegal, when we practice reflection regularly, in addition to maintaining integrative caring and connecting relationships, we can stimulate the growth of the integrative fibers of the brain. These fibers allow you to have resilience.

Mindfulness-Based Stress Reduction (MBSR) strategies are practiced and taught in health care facilities, yoga studios, prisons, law firms, and schools. Mindfulness isn't a religion, a disciplinary tool, meditation, or the absence of thought, nor is it simply calmness or happiness. Regular daily mindfulness practice has been shown to reduce stress and anxiety, improve attention, impulse control and regulation, increase empathy and understanding of others, and promote a sense of calm and the ability to be present to yourself and others. Many, if not all, of these benefits can positively affect teaching and learning.

Mindfulness Starts with You

According to *mindfulschools.org*, "When teachers learn mindfulness, they not only reap personal benefits such as reduced stress and burnout, but their schools do as well. In randomized controlled trials, teachers who learned mindfulness reported greater efficacy in doing their jobs and had more emotionally supportive classrooms and better classroom organization based on independent observations." With regular mindfulness practice, you can transform your busy classroom into a learning sanctuary where the mind and body are in sync. In large part because I've been consistently practicing mindfulness, the past two years of teaching have been the calmest, most engaging, and genuinely rewarding in my twenty-year career.

Mindfulness practice may also help you elevate your performance. Stress and anxiety are inevitable during the school year, and they can scatter our attention. While we're still "performing" our duties in terms of delivering content, we have to ask ourselves, "Are we really fully present to hear what students are saying and not saying in their answers?" We may be missing their small cues, teachable moments, and opportunities to engage in thoughtful conversation. Scheduled mindfulness practice can help us avoid simply going through the motions. With repeated practice, we can recognize in advance when we're not at our best and self-regulate at an elevated level to reach our potential.

Personally practicing mindfulness is also important so we can notice exactly what each child needs in order to be prepared both mentally and physically for engaged learning. Additionally, when we are practicing mindfulness and modeling it to our students, we can explicitly teach lifelong mindfulness strategies to them.

Creating a ritual of morning mindfulness has helped me face each school day with confidence and positivity. What do your mornings typically look like? Do you spend your morning juggling multiple household tasks while rushing to squeeze in a morning workout class, fight traffic, and get to school on time? If so, develop some proactive "pregame" teaching mindfulness rituals on your way to school. Practice yoga before school or practice mindful breathing at stop lights, focusing on the air slowly inhaling through your nose and slowly exhaling through your mouth. Listen to mellow music on your drive to work, focusing on the musical instruments, or sing your favorite positive song as loudly as you can. These activities will empower you with focus and positivity as you greet your students who are arriving from their own morning rituals.

As the school day continues, it's important to notice your pace and momentum. You may be dragging from exhaustion, having your PR ("personal record") teaching day, or getting caught up in the busyness of the day, trying to push beyond what you can realistically achieve on your endless "to do" list. When I'm rushing through the day, I stop to remind myself that daily demands don't dictate the speed at which I operate. If we typically rush from one school activity to the next, we may miss important opportunities to connect with students or give them the extra encouragement or added challenge they need.

Mindfulness gives us the perfect quick opportunity to check in and potentially lower our blood pressure with mindful breathing. We may discover we need to make thoughtful, purposeful changes in order to refocus to be more engaged in our teaching.

Bringing It to the Classroom

I talked previously about your morning ritual, but what about your students' morning routines? We have no idea what they are like. Did your students eat breakfast? Was there a parent helping them get ready for their day of learning, were the students getting their parents out of bed, or was there even a parent in their home? Learners come to school from a variety of environments, and it's likely that many of them are highly stressful. While we don't always know our learners' individual circumstances, we know for sure they can't easily absorb information when they are too tired, distracted, or in a state of fight-or-flight.

For some students, school may provide relief from the stress of home and can be the best environment to help them slow down, connect, and focus on learning. For other students, school can be a daunting and anxious place. I see smiling students walk in and out of my classroom but, during the day, learning challenges can arise, activating the fight-or-flight instinct, causing those smiling fourth grade faces to fade. When this happens, thinking and problem-solving become more difficult.

As teachers, we have a unique opportunity to notice these signals and provide students with tools and strategies to manage their stress and regulate their emotions. Daily mindfulness practice may also help students develop self-awareness, improve academic achievement, and improve both interpersonal and intrapersonal skills. With daily practice this can create a strong foundation where great learning can take place. Students may also become more aware of positive traits such as empathy, kindness, generosity, and gratitude, which can be trained and strengthened in and out of the classroom through mental training, coaching, and whole group practice.

As you begin developing your personal mindfulness practice, try practicing the student mindfulness activities below. Take time to reflect on how you feel before, during, and after the activities. Notice how they help you and think about how they may help your students. Practice these strategies independently. Additionally, consider taking mindfulness classes, watching reputable videos, going on a mindfulness retreat, or asking your principal to allow someone like me to conduct a professional development session. The most important part of bringing mindfulness to school is practicing these strategies authentically and regularly before you teach them to your students. From this point, the quality of your connection with your students and how you teach these lessons will truly make the biggest impact on their learning.

If you choose to teach mindfulness strategies to your students as standalone lessons or as brain break transitions, it's important to first discuss it with your administration and provide proven research-based outcomes, as well as how your personal practice positively affects your teaching. If your administration supports you, it's also important to share this information with other teachers and the parents of your students. Finally, before teaching mindfulness strategies, provide your students with a clear definition and purpose of mindfulness and a context of what mindlessness may look like in a classroom. If you are concerned about your ability to concretely understand mindfulness and clearly communicate it to your administration, fellow teachers, and your students and their parents, or if you are simply interested in learning more about the science behind mindfulness, including the parts of the brain, their function and how they are connected, please visit *eduninja.net* for more about the neuroscience behind mindfulness and learning.

Getting Started

Make mindfulness a daily habit in your classroom to give everyone time to check in to the exact moment, without judgment, to notice what is happening. Mindfulness takes just minutes and can be scheduled first thing in the morning, right after recess, or during a lunch club. Scheduling daily mindfulness at the same time every day ensures it doesn't get missed.

While mindfulness isn't intended to be used to produce a calmer, more peaceful class environment, this is often the nice byproduct of it. After taking a moment to check in, notice their natural breath, focus on slowing it down and, in turn, reduce their heart rate, students often notice a calmer, more focused internal and external state where better learning may occur.

How beautiful it would be for students in your classroom to notice when they're feeling anxious, unfocused, or distracted and, at different times throughout the day, without anyone even knowing, to be able to stop and practice some mindful breathing when they need it most. Mindfulness makes it possible and realistic for students to take on new challenges with a refreshed, refocused mindset. When you model these lifelong learning strategies and give students opportunities to develop them, mindfulness becomes part of your classroom culture.

Simple, Beginner Mindfulness Lessons

The following examples are fast and easy mindfulness lessons you can use as a brain break, during classroom transition time, before a test, or in a lunch club.

Mindful Body Posture and Breathing Awareness

Purpose

Students will notice how they hold their body, how their body feels when they are at rest, and their breathing. They will become aware of their part in the overall classroom learning environment. This body posture will be used in most mindfulness practices.

Hook

Share with students a very specific time when you recognized your thoughts were scattered or you were multitasking, sleepy, or on autopilot. Share how you used mindful breathing, with your eyes open, in this situation—perhaps in a yoga class, or in the classroom at recess. Let students know how they can use this strategy in many different environments to notice how they are feeling, how their body feels, and how slowing their breathing may lower their heart rate if they are "revved up."

Process

1. Have students sit quietly at their desks with their shoulders back, torso purposefully straight but not forced. Invite students to close their eyes and place their hands on their lap. Remind them (especially those on Swiss Balls) to sit still and be still.

2. Have students place one hand on their heart and one on their stomach.

3. Have students notice and feel the rise and fall of their chest and stomach as they are breathing in through their nose and out through their mouth. This can be for thirty seconds, initially, and up to a minute or two with practice.

4. You may let students breathe on their own or lead the whole class in a guided breathing exercise. (I like to lead a whole class breathing exercise when we're beginning.)

5. Ring a bell and invite students to open their eyes. Ask students what they noticed about their body, breath, etc. before, during, and after practicing mindfulness. Ask them when this mindfulness strategy would be good to use and why.

6. Follow up with a quick class discussion and/or a few minutes of journaling.

Mindful Listening

Purpose

Students will be able to focus and notice sounds better. This awareness can help students in many areas, such as science observations, music, sports, listening to directions, etc.

Hook

Talk about a time when you sat in an environment, perhaps in a garden, and just noticed the immediate sounds, like the birds chirping or people talking in the distance. Then share about sitting in silence for a bit and how you started hearing sounds like the humming of a bird's wings as it flew by.

Process

Build upon the mindful body awareness lesson.

1. Ask students to sit quietly at their desks with their shoulders back and their torso purposefully straight, but not forced. Invite them to close their eyes and put their hands on their laps. Remind students (especially those on Swiss Balls) to sit still.

2. Tell students the focus is "mindful listening." Their job will be to just listen.

3. Ring a bell and have students listen to the bell in its entirety and notice when they can't hear it anymore.

4. Direct their attention to other sounds. After thirty seconds to a minute, ring a bell and ask students what other sounds they heard.

5. Invite students to close their eyes again and see if they notice any new sounds, perhaps from their bodies, the classroom, neighboring classrooms, or the school hallway. Allow students to listen for thirty seconds but, eventually, they can build up stamina to listen a minute or two.

6. Ask students what new sounds they heard the second time.

7. Follow up with a quick class discussion and/or a few minutes of journaling.

Mindful Listening Strategy Reminders for Students

Being a mindful listener means practicing self-awareness to notice both internal and external distractions and then selecting the best strategy to help you refocus. The following are some excellent reminders to include in your mindful listening practice with your students.

- Sometimes before I listen to a speaker, I will take a few minutes to practice mindful breathing with my eyes open as he is getting ready to address the group. This refocuses my mind and my body.

- When the speaker is speaking, I give her my full attention, including making eye contact. The speaker's words are my main focus.
- Sometimes when I find my mind wandering to a past or future thought, I try focusing on a sensation in my body such as how the back of my legs feel as they are pressed against the ground. This brings me back to the present moment so I can reconnect to the speaker's words.
- Sometimes I need to readjust my legs as I am sitting for a while listening to a speaker. I use this physical cue to refocus my mental concentration as well.
- If I notice a student whispering, I name it "distraction" in my mind and redirect my attention to the speaker. If the whispering continues, I can ask the student politely to stop or tell the teacher.
- If I want the speaker to know I'm listening, I can show respect by smiling and nodding, being aware of my body posture.
- I can ask questions in my head and, when there is an opportunity, I can paraphrase by saying *I noticed you said …* or *I wonder …* or to clarify for understanding, I can ask, *Did you mean …*
- If I find myself losing focus, I can try practicing empathetic listening, putting myself in the speaker's shoes and asking myself a question from her perspective. For example, "I wonder what it would be like to be a forty-two-year-old teaching fourth graders how to add fractions with unlike denominators while they are having side conversations or looking around the room?"

- If I get distracted, I can refocus on the speaker's purpose and ask myself, *What is he trying to teach me* or *When would this lesson be important for me to use?*

Mindful Movement

Purpose

By focusing on each micro movement, students will become aware of the environment they are in or are entering and how they are moving in it.

Hook

Share personal stories of times you used mindful movement. For example, I share with students how I notice each micromovement of my foot on the slackline, feeling how it moves from heel to toe during every single step; or I'll share how, when rock climbing, I don't just focus on my hand and foot placement, but I focus on the point on the hold I touch with the tip of my toe or the place I grab with my fingers or fingertips. Each and every movement is purposeful and focused.

Process

1. As students walk into the classroom, ask them what they notice about the environment and how they are moving through the space.
2. As students transition from one subject to another, to and from recess, or when walking on campus, ask them to notice what it feels and looks like to transition mindfully.
3. Follow up with a quick class discussion about when this would be a good strategy to use and/or give them a few minutes to journal, reviewing this strategy and thinking about how they can use it again or share it with others.

Mindful Guided Box Breathing

Purpose

By focusing attention on each inhale and exhale, students will become aware of their current concentration, finding ways to increase concentration and possibly reduce stress.

Hook

Share a personal story of when you used Mindful Box Breathing, maybe before giving a speech, competing in an athletic competition, or during a performance. For example, I often stare stories with my class of how I use mindful breathing before speaking in front of audiences, balancing high across a new Ninja obstacle, or serving a volleyball for a critical game point.

Box breathing is not a new technique, but it is an effective tool to help stay calm, focused, and centered. Used by a variety of people including elite military personnel, law enforcement officers, yoga practitioners, keynote speakers, athletes, and students in classrooms, with regular practice, this breathing technique may help improve concentration, lower heart rate, lower blood pressure, reduce stress, and help both teachers and students with emotional regulation. Our class practices box breathing in situations where students may feel anxious, such as before a test or a presentation.

Process

1. Draw a square on a poster or the whiteboard.
2. Label the four sides, starting at the top and moving clockwise. Inhale four seconds, hold four seconds, exhale four seconds, hold four seconds. Draw one arrow on each side moving clockwise.

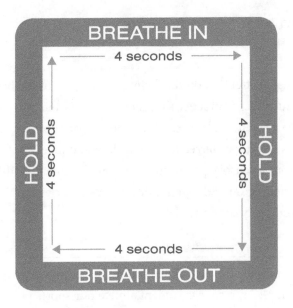

3. Point to the diagram, explaining each side of the box while you model the breathing. On the first side, inhale through your nose as you slowly count to four. On the second side of the box, hold your breath as you slowly count to four. On the third side, exhale through your mouth as you slowly count to four, and on the final side hold your breath again as you slowly count to four.

4. Lead younger students through the box breathing with their eyes open so they can see the visual. If you're working with older students, you may guide them through the exercise with their eyes closed.

5. Repeat this cycle two or three times.

6. Follow up with a quick class discussion, asking students when this would be a good strategy to use, and/or give them a few minutes to journal, reviewing this strategy and thinking about when they could use it again or share it with others.

Guided Mindful Body Scan

Purpose

By focusing attention on the feeling in one part of the body at a time, students will practice the art of awareness and how the body feels. As a result, students can train their capacity to pay attention (which can be transferred to classwork) and notice how the body feels from a sensory perspective without judgment or thinking, strengthening our EduNinja mindfulness muscles and noticing the mind-body connection.

Hook

Share personal stories of times you used the body scan exercise. For example, as a college student athlete our sports psychologist would, from time to time, take us through this body scan exercise after practice. With the body scan skills introduction, I've since made it a weekly practice when teaching EduNinja™ Fit. It's a lifelong skill I will always practice.

Process

1. This activity can be taught with students seated or lying face up on individual mats. I like guiding students in a mindful body scan practice during the end of our EduNinja™ Fit session so they can be lying on their backs.
2. Invite students to close their eyes and visualize themselves on a secluded beach. Tell them to hear the sounds, take in the scents, and look at the scenery. You can expand on each of these with more details for a couple of minutes.
3. When students are relaxed, guide them through a two- to three-minute body scan, starting with their feet and working up to their heads.

4. Direct students' attention to their feet. Instruct them to squeeze their feet tightly for three seconds and then direct them to let go. Redirect their attention to their calves and repeat, squeezing for three seconds and then letting go. Move up the body, repeating this process with thighs, bottom, stomach, lower back, chest, arms, shoulders, hands, and, finally, tell them to scrunch their face and relax.

5. Invite students to notice how they feel and how their body feels.

6. You could have a quick class discussion, asking them when this might be a good strategy to use, and/or they could record their new learning in their journal.

More Mindfulness Activities

Mindful Journaling

You may choose to transition to your writing block with a thirty-second to two-minute mindfulness strategy and then follow up with a few minutes of reflective journal writing. You might also want the class to write based on an optional prompt:

- What did you feel in your mind and body before (during and/or after) mindfulness practice today?
- What do you notice about our classroom environment when we practice mindfulness?
- In what other situations might you be able to practice this mindfulness strategy?
- When and where could you schedule mindfulness practice times at home?
- Who could you teach these mindfulness strategies to who would benefit from them?

Gratitude Journal

During November, students start keeping a daily gratitude journal, sharing what people they are grateful for and why they're better because of them. Then, students write about specific ways they can be like their mentors for someone else. Each school day starts with students spending just a few minutes writing their gratitude and a daily quote from a list I've gathered over the years. Students can make connections and develop deeper meaning. They are also encouraged to share their own favorite quotes or their gratitude for classmates during class meeting time.

Class Meetings

Our class has weekly "meetings" where we sit in a circle so everyone can be seen and heard. These provide opportunities for a number of things. For example, students practice sharing and receiving compliments (very teachable moments at the elementary level especially). Students can also look to one another for solutions to playground issues or proactive strategies for reaching peaceful resolutions. For some, the meetings simply provide a chance to be heard with anything that may be troubling them.

Class meetings provide an excellent opportunity to share a new strategy with students. For example, students occasionally feel angry on the playground. Using "I statements" is an excellent strategy for students during these times:

"**I feel** sad **when** my classmates exclude me from foursquare. **I wish** they would include me so I can play a game I love just as much as they do."

During these meetings, students can discuss purposely picking appropriate mindful strategies. Instead of saying something mindlessly hurtful or getting angry, students can choose to try practicing mindful breathing and then talking about what upset them. They may also choose to ignore the situation and walk away, journal about it, talk to a trusted person, or bring it to the class meeting. Your class may come up with other strategies they can note on a class poster and/or in their journals. You can easily do follow-up lessons on how students can notice when intense emotions are coming on in their bodies. For example, when they notice their cheeks feeling hot and their body temperature rising, they recognize they are getting mad and know it's time to try an appropriate strategy.

Class meetings are also great times for brainstorming ways we can help our school and the greater community. Maybe your students want to make fun, educational posters of healthy "superpower" veggies to encourage elementary students to make healthier choices in the lunch line. Or maybe your class will decide to run in a race supporting a cause you believe in, or maybe you will want to create your own fundraiser. The opportunities are endless.

Voting on upcoming outside-of-class field trips is another excellent use of class meeting time. These field trips can be the bonding glue in relationships with students and families. They also help build trust, genuine friendships, and mutual respect, plus students talk about and remember field trips forever. Class meetings are a great place for picture book read-alouds, class discussions, and poster making or journaling to practice mindfulness. No matter what you use your class meeting time for, students are consistently engaging in reflective activity and building a lifelong skill.

Mindful Speaking Strategy Reminders for Students

Being a mindful speaker means practicing self-awareness to ensure you are accurately communicating your thoughts and ideas while also considering the needs of the listener. The following are some excellent reminders to share with your students.

- Before I speak, I pause and carefully choose my words to authentically capture what I want to say in a truthful, respectful way by considering the other person's feelings. I may ask, "Is it true? Is it kind?"
- I don't just say what other people want to hear; instead, I speak from my heart.
- If I lose my focus when I'm speaking, I can reconnect to my breath or a feeling in my body to regain my focus.
- I check in to ensure I am speaking at an acceptable speed and not rushing, clearly enunciating my words, and using words my listeners understand. I also take time to "read the faces" of my audience to see if I need to explain something.

Mindfulness Checklist and Strategies

As noted earlier, the most important part of bringing mindfulness to your students is to personally practice these strategies and use them authentically. However, to equip your students with lifelong mindfulness tools, you have to do more than simply use them personally. You have to explicitly teach mindfulness skills, naming, in front of your students, how you are actively feeling, what you are thinking about and reflecting on, and how you are actively choosing your actions despite any outside conditions. For example:

> My chest feels heavy and tight right now. I feel a little anxious about a deadline for a big project. I want to feel lighter, and I don't want to worry about the deadline. If I practice box breathing, I will mindfully take bigger breaths and exhale fully. This will calm my body and my mind as I focus on my breath entering and leaving my lungs. When I return to my learning, I'm focused on what's in front of me and ready to learn.

Consider the following checklist to ensure you are intention-ally modeling mindfulness strategies and giving your students every opportunity to build skills they can use in your classroom and throughout their lives.

- Do you and your students have opportunities to practice mindfulness daily in your classroom?
- Are you leading whole-class mindfulness practices or coach-ing while you are conferring with students throughout the day?
- Is the physical classroom environment conducive to stu-dent self-regulation? Do students have opportunities to use self-regulation scaffolding tools until they are truly self-reg-ulating? For example, could you hang a poster on the wall asking, "How are you feeling?" or "What are you noticing right now?" or "What do you need to do your best learning?" As you teach a new mindfulness strategy, list it on the poster as a resource or reminder.
- Do students have a cumulative list (in their journal or on a classroom poster) of physical and emotional feelings and EduNinja empowering strategies? For example:

    I feel...

    Tired: sleepy, sluggish, stuck, bored, slow

    Focused: engaged in my learning and conversations; in the flow

    Overstimulated: antsy, like I want to run and jump

    I can practice these EduNinja empowering strategies:

    - *Mindful Breathing*
    - *Mindful Movement*
    - *Mindful Box Breathing*
    - *Mindful Body Scan*

- *Grateful Journaling*
- *Name Your Emotion*
- *Respond vs. React*

Questions to Consider

- Do you need to give up some control to let individual students use some appropriate movement strategies during periods of independent learning?
- Do you notice and coach in when needed to help your learners make correct self-regulation choices for themselves and others in their learning environment?
- Do you provide mindfulness reflection time for journaling and whole class discussion? How often?
- Do you model simple self-regulation strategies for students? Don't be afraid to stop and say to the class, "I'm feeling so _____ now. I know I need to do _____ to refocus on my teaching or learning."
- Do you explicitly model for students response flexibility, the capacity to pause and consider options before taking action?

Remember that it's hard for students to learn when they are too tired or overstimulated or in fight-or-flight mode. Check in with your students to ensure they are in the "sweet zone" of learning. Notice when they need your help to point them to ways they can recognize how their body feels and choose an appropriate mindfulness strategy.

By mindfully observing your students, you may begin to notice the small cues showing they are engaged in the task at hand, or the cues revealing their mind is elsewhere. For one student, tapping her fingers on her desk shows she is distracted, while the same movement helps another student get his work done. You might also notice an overstimulated student bouncing rapidly on the Swiss Ball or another student sitting at her desk with a clenched jaw. These noticings provide a great context for teaching mindfulness strategies.

Keep the following mindfulness strategies in mind as you encounter these teachable moments with individual students or small groups of students. They are also great reminders for your own personal mindfulness practice!

Pay attention. Attention can be increased through training or practice. Notice when your attention is scattered from physically and mentally multi-tasking. Focus on your breath to bring awareness to the present moment. Be a kind observer of the mind.

Respond instead of react. Calm breathing triggers the parasympathetic nervous system (the opposite of the fight-or-flight response), which slows heart rate and makes blood pressure go down. We can create space between the emotion and the response using response flexibility, focusing on breathing to lengthen this time in order to spot an impulse ("I'm about to get angry") before we act. With practice, we can also choose to notice the sensory perception of an emotion (tight chest or hot face) and name it ("anger") in order to give ourselves time to pick an appropriate response.

Choose how to act when you are emotional. Identify your triggers and make a plan to either prevent situations from escalating or deal with them when they arise. Remember to calm your mind, focus on your breathing, do a full body scan, name the emotion, and pick your response.

Show compassion. Showing compassion for someone we find difficult is challenging. Realize everyone is doing the best he can. Tune in to the other person's perspective to understand why she may be acting a certain way. Most likely her action isn't about you. Look for the context and have compassion for it. Can you try shifting your perspective and emotional state before you interact with the person by coming from a place of wonder or curiosity, asking, "I wonder why this person is really acting this way? What is the underlying emotion and why? How can I remember to not take these words or actions personally?"

Do an activity that makes you happy. Notice when you slip into the "mindlessly getting things done phase" or a fight-or-flight response. You may be working too hard and stress may be building up. Your body may be saying you need a break. Stop and ask yourself, "What am I noticing and what do I need? What makes me happy?" Then pick an activity off your list (yoga, hot shower, massage, walk in nature, hot tea, meet up with friends, etc.) and go do it. This will likely give you strength and a baseline to return to.

Perform a full body scan. Mindfully listen to your body through a full body scan. Direct your attention to various parts of your body as you tighten and release muscles.

Be in the moment. In sports, art, music, and other arenas, people talk about being "in the flow." Practice focusing on the moment-to-moment process rather than the outcome. If you start thinking too much about the outcome, you will not be in the flow and, most likely, will "choke" and not perform well. Focus on the micromovements of the skill rather than on winning or failing (remember the slackline). Be fully present. Let the outcomes take care of themselves.

Be a kind observer of the mind. Stop judging yourself and others and start "noticing" things instead. With practice, you may even start trusting your intuition.

Notice distractions and refocus. Model for students how to name internal distractions (thoughts or feelings) and external distractions (another student playing with an eraser or sharpening a pencil). Remind them to name their own distractions and then refocus. You can also model distracting feelings in your physical body, name them, and then refocus on the task at hand. You may need to explicitly model this strategy multiple times before students truly see it, hear it, practice it, and develop the skill personally. Students can also redirect their attention to their breath when they notice distractions. It's also important for students to know that, even though they may experience a sense of calm when they practice mindfulness, there may be times when thoughts and certain emotions distract them—even when they're trying to focus on something specific, such as their breathing. Remind them this is okay.

Authentically model mindfulness. Students need to observe how you are authentically using mindfulness as a tool. Model it by telling them, "Wow, I'm starting to feel frustrated with the choices some students are making while I'm talking. I could use a moment of mindfulness. Would you like to join me?"

"Coach In" to Redirect Student Focus. Use situations from your classroom to coach in, leading students through mindful practice. For example, if your students are noisy during a transition, say to them, "I notice a lot of loud noise during this transition to math. Maybe moving mindfully would help. What does mindful movement look like? What does it sound like? What does it feel like? How do you know what it looks, sounds, and feels like?" Practice with the bell and/or mindful breathing. Challenge students to listen for different sounds as they walk into a "quiet" classroom. They may notice the clock ticking or the faint voices from the classroom next door. Without mindfulness these sounds would go unnoticed. Plus, you have quieter students walking into your classroom.

Flex Your EduNinja Muscles

★ What strategies can you adopt to avoid multitasking and doing things fast paced? How can you feel calm and relaxed in a learning environment where quality work and learning engagement is the norm? How can you bring more mindfulness to your interactions with others? To your daily routines? How can you identify triggers and develop a plan for responding to them?

★ What are some things you may notice when you check in? (Remember to notice without judging). You might notice some of the following examples:

   ★ I'm grateful for all the support I'm receiving.

   ★ I feel anxious since I ended up drinking four cups of coffee this morning.

   ★ My hamstrings are tight from the extra mile I ran last night.

   ★ I feel energized when I get to spend time with my friends.

   ★ I'm exhausted since I stayed up an hour later last night.

   ★ I'm thinking ahead to all the things on my "to do list" I won't be able to get done.

   ★ My hips finally feel open after last night's yoga class.

   ★ I feel overwhelmed because . . .

★ How could mindfulness help you and your classroom community of learners have the best year yet?

An EduNinja
Embodies Grit

*We are what we repeatedly do. Excellence,
then, is not an act, but a habit.*

—Aristotle

*Every morning you have two choices:
continue to sleep with your dreams
or wake up and go chase them.*

—Unknown

Do you have grit?

Grit is persistence and resilience. Grit isn't training just to sprint through one obstacle or one obstacle course. Grit means having the determination and stamina to run, balance, climb up and over obstacles, fall—and then get up to do it over and over again. Grit is focusing on effort—not outcome—and giving your best effort every single time. When people talk about grit in education or athletics, the idea is about working hard enough and long enough, no matter your ability. It's three full years of training equating to zero playing time.

Psychologist Angela Duckworth offered this definition of grit in her 2013 TED Talk:

Grit is passion and perseverance for very long-term goals. Grit is having stamina. Grit is sticking with your future day in, day out. Not just for the week. Not just for the month, but for years, and working really hard to make that future a reality. Grit is living life like it is a marathon, not a sprint.

I agree with her that grit takes overall perseverance over an extended amount of time, but I firmly believe great performers also work in sprints too. Great performers work in short bursts with an intensity that can't be sustained over a long period of time to make big gains, recover purposefully, and train sustainably. Then they train with intensity all over again, to elevate to another level while battling obstacles and setbacks over a long period of time.

Grit involves connecting your purpose and passions at work while serving others. It's pursuing something against all odds, not letting anyone or any situation overcome you. You dig deep and find ways to rise from your "splashes into the water" to do even better because you know you can. As a "gritty" EduNinja, you are proactive in your application of strategies because you've already done the envisioning work in the lessons, and you're applying the flexibility to anticipate and overcome unexpected obstacles. You don't stop until you're proud.

I picture grit being modeled by military personnel and first responders who sacrifice countless hours as servant leaders. But teachers are servant leaders who also dig deep to connect passion and purpose and push on with mental and physical strength to better serve others. We live it daily—and love it most days. And even during my toughest weeks of grading essays, writing report card comments, creating curriculum, helping students with disagreements, and pre-paring for parent conferences, I realize my challenges are absolutely nothing compared to how military personnel and first responders, and even other teachers, are constantly being challenged both mentally and physically in their environments. When I have too many respon-sibilities, I just step back, check in, and put things in perspective.

When I feel like quitting, I come back to my purpose and reason why I teach: to share what I learned from my mentors in order to help others achieve their own personal greatness by giving their best effort daily, living a healthy, happy lifestyle, and helping others. I review my mindset and make a plan to either slow down (with some relaxing reg-gae or Native American flute tunes) or push the accelerator to achieve more (cranking up old school heavy metal or Skrillex). If doubt or negativity tries to creep in, I just glance at the positive notes around my house to remind me what grit is. For example, if my EduNinja mindset isn't turned on yet in the morning or if I'm exhausted and don't want to work out, I recall Coach Rose's words ("You always have to be ready to go") or look at the note near my coffee maker, "Don't let your hands get soft," reminding me to get to the gym. When I walk into my classroom, I'm reminded of grit again by posters stating, "Don't stop until you're proud," "Do something today your future self will thank you for," and "Mistakes are proof you're trying."

Modeling Grit

Our job is to model grit throughout the day for our students and colleagues. We start by giving our best effort every day, no matter what. It may also mean sharing with your students how you wake up at 5:00 a.m. to work out, write a book, prepare food for your fam-ily, feed your pets, or work on a big project before your school day even starts. This gives them a new perspective about sustained daily grit—grit needed before, during, and after school to achieve passion-ate goals in all areas of your life.

Coach John Wooden was a pioneer, a maverick, and a real EduNinja. He wasn't *just* a three-time All-American basketball player at Purdue University or a high school English teacher or the head coach at UCLA. During his time as an English teacher and high school coach, Wooden developed and shared his philosophy of success with students and athletes. He modeled giving ourselves time to become "good" when striving for "greatness" by not quitting if we're not "suc-cessful" in our first year, fifth year, or even fifteenth year. We all want instant gratification, but these lessons take time to learn. Developing patience along with skill is part of the process. Coach Wooden credits what he learned and practiced as a teacher for the success he carried over into his college coaching career—winning ten NCAA national championships in a twelve-year period as head coach at UCLA—*after* sixteen years of coaching. I guarantee most people would have given up way before then and never discovered their own greatness. Not John Wooden. He lived and modeled his philosophy of success as a basketball player, teacher, and coach.

Clearly define and model for students your philosophy of success while encouraging them to develop and showcase their own defini-tion. Just like John Wooden modeled for us, we should be "making each day our masterpiece," having the courage to put in the daily hard work despite any obstacles.

Clearly define and model for students your philosophy of success while encouraging them to develop and showcase their own definition.

What does it take to develop this kind of grit and determination to achieve our bigger goals in all areas of our lives? It takes a good monitoring system to ensure we're meeting the needs in each area and constantly reaching up to meet those ever-rising goals. If we feel stuck in any area, maybe it's time to raise the bar!

Bringing It to the Classroom

We have a great opportunity to teach our students to develop their own grit. Consider the following as you take advantage of this opportunity in your classrooms.

Model grit. Teachers need to model grit daily. It isn't a once-a-week activity; the whole point of grit is to live it and model it every minute. Your students respect you and watch how you do everything. They will want to follow your example when they see you giving your best effort on even the smallest of things. You can also gently remind them you know how they feel when they want to give up. Share your story and show how you eventually grew from the experience by changing your mindset and overcoming the obstacle you were faced with.

Model failure. We also need to model failure regularly. Students need to see us giving our best effort even when we're not succeeding. They need to see us come back and find ways to learn from our mistakes and become better. We need to share personal stories daily of how we work our hardest and fail as part of our everyday lives. This can easily be incorporated into read-aloud discussions about character traits or as we apply new math curriculum strategies we weren't taught in grade school. Teachers can share so many different stories about trying to learn new technology in professional development, or stories of trying to learn specific lessons as a child, or maybe about trying for weeks to master a new yoga pose and finally achieving it because you were persistent.

Students need to see us giving our best effort even when we're not succeeding. They need to see us come back and find ways to learn from our mistakes and become better.

As an EduNinja, I have plenty of failures to share with students. I've found my students connect with me and feel more comfortable attempting a challenge and failing when they know I've fallen off a bouldering wall and landed on a crash mat multiple times before finally getting it. I've shown my students I may get ripped hands or a few bruises, but with problem-solving and persistence, anything is possible, and nothing is like the glorious moment when you finally "get it" as a learner.

Model positive phrases. No matter where we are in the process of using the EduNinja mindset, explicitly modeling positive phrases for our students helps us raise the bar to new levels of achievement for them. It all begins with mindset. Be explicit when teaching and make comments like these an important part of your lesson or small group instruction:

- Some students may say __, but Little Ninjas say __.
- I'm not good at this **yet**, but I'm getting better.
- I love challenges because they make me better.

These prompts create a culture for developing and reinforcing the "grit and commit" EduNinja mindset. Students use them to reflect on how it feels and looks to get something wrong multiple times, build upon their attempts, and see how they can improve by using new strategies. Whole class discussions help other students see authentic examples of real grit from their classmates. Be consistent in highlighting this and making student reflection an important part of your classroom.

Try these EduNinja mindset phrases in your personal life so you have authentic classroom examples to share with your students. Reflection is an important piece of "gritting and committing" to your goals.

Reward effort. We need to praise the daily effort exhibited by students that may lead (or eventually lead) to a desired outcome or learning progress. We need to let students know that we appreciate their effort and their focus despite what others may perceive as "good" or "bad" assessment scores. We could say, "I noticed you tried multiple math strategies until you got the answer," or "I noticed you completed this reading test with full focus by rereading and fully answering all parts of the question. These strategies may lead to successful answers." On the contrary, you can point out when students may need to give more effort. "I noticed you completed this project quickly and accurately. I wonder if you could pick a more challenging option next time?"

Provide opportunities for practice. We need to provide leveled opportunities to push students just beyond their comfort zone, so that they fail multiple times before getting the correct answer. They also need to become comfortable with being uncomfortable by developing positive self-talk, first with our coaching and, eventually, independently. We need to coach students in small groups where we're able to ask thought-provoking questions without giving hints, so students can start asking themselves these same questions. Teachers also need to coach students on how they should encourage their peers to succeed by asking thought-provoking questions to help promote the grit and growth mindset. For example, in our classroom community of learners, our class grit comes from our definition of being a "Little Ninja." As a community of "Little Ninjas," we encourage our classmates with positive words of encouragement and thought-provoking questions when they're temporarily failing so they can have their mind-blowing learning moment. We don't deprive them of their learning opportunity by giving them the answer.

Teach willpower. Willpower is the ability to do things now your future self will thank you for. It's doing the things you might not necessarily want to do at this moment in order to strive for achieving bigger goals. Students need to see their teachers practicing willpower explicitly, and teachers need to offer opportunities for students to practice willpower. They need to feel this and reflect on the process to develop this lifelong habit. Proudly share examples of willpower strategies you use during the school day as a teacher and lifelong learner. Don't forget to share "nonexamples" of willpower and the results of them.

Demonstrate how mindset affects learning. It's important for teachers to show students how mindset affects learning. I keep anecdotal notes of mindset statements students have at the beginning of a lesson, new unit of study, or the beginning of the school year. As a unit progresses, I ask students how positive self-talk or mindset affected their learning and growth. I may say, "I noticed you were originally saying 'I'm not good at math.' and now you're saying 'I'm really proud of my effort, and I can do long division now.' What does this make you think?"

Share these achievements individually when conferring personally with a student or in a whole group setting so other students can learn and be inspired. Share on report cards both positive mindset and grit development shown in students' daily work habits or in their speech, so parents can also see how much their child's mindset affects learning in a positive way. Parents can then help promote these same positive habits at home.

Educate parents too. Don't forget to educate parents about grit by sharing the learning opportunities you are providing in the classroom and the thought prompts you are using to help students develop grit, so parents can provide similar situations and coaching at home. You can share these during Back to School Night, parent conferences, weekly emails, and positive phone calls home.

With daily practice your class will be proud to be "Little Ninjas" or "Little Champions"—whatever your awesome group is called— because every unique member will have a clear set of community expectations. Your class will have a teacher modeling grit daily, classmates showing their best effort and saying positive EduNinja mindset statements, and students encouraging others to strive for personal greatness and awesome learning moments.

Refine the Goals and Action Plan

When we raise the bar, students may take a bit longer to reach the goal, meaning there are missed goals along the way. Goals can be missed for a few reasons, so it's important to take time to reflect daily on how to approach new tasks or new attempts at a goal. Think about the goal you missed and ask some questions to see why you fell short. Make a new plan to elevate.

- Did you take time to clearly define your personal legacy or big goal? Did you use clear, decisive, positive, and measurable words when setting your goals with soul? Did you fully think through or envision what the big goal looks like or feels like?

- Was your big goal broken down into measurable, manageable steps? Could you add a quantity or a timeframe? Did you include all the parts of a SMART goal?
- Did you schedule or devote enough focused time on the priorities needed to be successful?
- Did you keep the promises you made to yourself about the practice strategies needed to stay on track and committed to your goal? How can you develop discipline and willpower through practice or asking help from a friend?
- Did you keep your mission statement front and center? How can you do this while maintaining balance in all other areas?
- How can you encourage and motivate yourself and others to be consistent in daily effort?
- How can you add flexibility in your thinking to accomplish tasks in a different way? A different time? With different people?

It's important for students to go through the process of honestly reflecting on their goals to see how they can refine them or their effort or strategies. Teaching mindfulness strategies to students may help them better notice the quality of their work as they're in the process of achieving their goals. To be successful and feel good about our effort in reaching our potential, we have to give our best effort day in and day out. We get tired, but we're building long-term stamina with the ability to eventually sprint through an obstacle course in a beautiful effortless flow. Visualize it. See it. Feel it. Live it!

Personal connections bring meaning and depth to our lives by providing a strong sense of love, belonging, and security. Additionally, there are numerous studies confirming the positive health benefits of belonging to a social network. We all know the feeling we get from an encouraging call from a friend or after reading an unforgettable and thoughtful handwritten letter from a student whose life, according to him or her, was forever changed in the most positive way with our help. Likewise, there's no better feeling than getting to "high five" or "fist bump" a student who finally gets a difficult math problem or your Ninja Warrior friend who finally gets the obstacle she's been working on for the last month. These moments are what matter the most. They are on the highlight reel when it comes to promoting a sense of community and making a positive impact for those around you.

Our positive impact is amplified when we bring attention to our similarities instead of our differences, connecting with others to see what's needed and how we can help in our own unique way. We all have different and wonderful talents to offer to help others strive for their personal greatness. Find your tribe and tap in to your immediate community and beyond by getting connected globally on social media. Start by surrounding yourself with like-minded individuals and social circles supporting healthy behaviors. Encourage others to do the same. Whether your group is based on school, faith, sports, arts, science, or environmental consciousness, we can all find connections to promote health and happiness in our schools and communities.

Promoting Wellness at School

Since we spend most of our time at school, doesn't it make sense to help create a positive, healthy school community for teachers, staff, students, and families? According to a 2015 Gallup Poll, only 30 percent of US teachers are engaged in their work. Could you imagine only 30 percent of your students being engaged in your lessons? Don't you think there's a huge correlation between teacher engagement and student engagement? You bet! Don't you think parents want their child's teachers to be engaged in their work? You bet!

We owe it to our students to practice personal healthy choices so we're at our best for our students, from getting to bed early, practicing a positive growth mindset, eating healthy and moving regularly throughout the day, to practicing mindfulness. We can lead by example so our students can learn these same healthy behaviors to become empowered and more engaged learners.

Many companies have stepped up to offer amazing health and wellness incentives and opportunities for their workers. It's time for our schools to do the same, but it's a collective effort and will not be sustained without the help of others. Look for ways you can encourage and promote increased employee engagement, well-being, productivity, workplace safety, and student engagement. Look for ways you could help add opportunities for nutrition, movement, or mindfulness. How can you possibly help teachers live healthier lives and potentially help in reducing absenteeism, turnover, workers' compensation claims, and disengaged teachers due to poor health?

If you're an administrator, you have an awesome opportunity to lead by example. Encourage and empower passionate teachers, staff, and families by looking at each person's strengths and inviting them to help in their own way. Classroom teachers, specials teachers, aids, staff personnel—everyone on campus can add an awesome perspective and a different way to contribute to a healthier campus.

Schedule opportunities for staff to connect on a regular basis to practice healthy habits. Plan fun events throughout the year for the entire school to train for. If you're promoting an upcoming 5K, you could practice vulnerability and the EduNinja mindset by telling yourself, "I'm going to start today by walking or jogging or running around the track during student PE class, so students and staff can see my lifelong dedication to health and well-being as a positive skill set." But don't stop there. Once you run the 5K, start training with your staff for the next event like #eduninja30. Fitness opportunities don't have to require people to be runners. Our class has monthly challenges involving push-ups, jumping rope, and other non-running activities. Maybe your school could have a similar variety of monthly challenges. Get creative and diverse in choosing fitness opportunities. Plan so everyone can participate at their own level of comfort throughout the entire year to build community.

If you're a teacher starting to add physical activity to your school day, maybe start by inviting a coworker, grade level team, or the entire staff to join you for morning yoga, recess walks, or afterschool workouts or hikes. If your fitness group is small with a few other teachers, focus on building consistency in those relationships and sharing your exercise consistency with other teachers and students at school. Don't give up, and don't get caught up in how many others join you. Just keep sharing what you're doing. Think about what you can do personally to build a stronger foundation of health and wellness at your school. Talk to your administrator and share the awesome things you've been doing to promote health and wellness. Share the benefits a healthier staff can provide for students. Your coworkers and you have a great power of positive influence within your school community. Tap into your synergy, practice consistency, and be a positive change to authentically build community.

When we practice being fit both mentally and physically on a daily basis, we become more actively engaged in our teaching, in our learning, and in our sense of community. This kinesthetic approach and the EduNinja mindset is my greatest "hook" for student learning. Because so many students play sports or watch them, they can relate to this. If you're just beginning your health and wellness journey, you can be a learner and go on the journey with your students. They may even get to shine by helping you. What an empowering experience for them! In the future, when your students come back to visit you, they'll remember these community activities of building healthy habits because of their emotional connection to health, wellness, and building your classroom, school, and global community.

Stay Connected

Teachers often get caught up in their overwhelming to-do lists, leading to isolation and a sense of loneliness. Building community is beneficial because it provides time and space to share your joys and challenges and find a fresh perspective to overcoming obstacles. Teaming up can help you solve problems or celebrate victories

> **Building community is beneficial because it provides time and space to share your joys and challenges and find a fresh perspective to overcoming obstacles.**

together. When others cheer you on, you may adopt confidence about achieving more together. When you look up to the people in your community, you may also increase your sense of self-worth as you connect to their positive influence and start applying similar healthy habits or positive acts. This interaction may boost your self-confidence and help others do the same. We all deserve to be loved, feel like we belong, and show love to everyone.

How can we stay connected in our teacher relationships on a regular basis? Could we commit to a weekly Twitter chat or meet for daily or weekly workouts, walks, or yoga? Consider starting a school garden, setting up a monthly staff healthy potluck lunch, or making daily healthy schoolwide announcements. Round up some teachers to support a local nonprofit by training together to run a race. The opportunities are endless as long as you focus on consistency to build those relationships.

A school community valuing health and wellness can produce significant positive changes around campus, such as healthy food options and empowered students making mindful food selections for healthier minds and bodies, happy teachers making movement and mindfulness part of their personal and professional practice, and healthy students enjoying sports in a variety of settings. These positive changes could spread to affect families as students share their new learning about healthy foods to buy at the grocery stores, mindfulness strategies, and exercises the whole family can do together. Together our school community can build a strong foundation of health and wellness for generations to come.

Tips for Working with
Your Administration

As teachers, we need to be modeling and using the same strategies to be at the top of our teaching game. When we do this, we know the positive benefits of movement and mindfulness in our lives. We also know those positive benefits may produce more focused students and better learners in our classrooms. Plus, there's also plenty of research-based evidence to support this. Now it's time to ask your administration to raise the bar to help students become healthier and achieve more.

Before talking to your principal or superintendent, do some homework so you know your school's potential needs, how activities can help, and several resources to help your school form a wellness team on campus (check out eduninja.net for a list). By reading this book, connecting with your community, visiting my blog, connecting with teachers online, and participating in the #eduninja30 30-Day Health and Wellness Challenge, you'll gather lots of ideas, resources, and potential community partnerships to share ideas with your administration. The goal is for students to make healthy food choices, exercise, and be mentally focused to do their best learning in school.

Before I talked to our superintendent about health and wellness for students, I used the Whole School, Whole Community, Whole Child (WSCC) Framework to advocate for student and teacher health and wellness. This framework states:

- Each student enters school healthy and learns about and practices a healthy lifestyle.
- Our school facility and environment support and reinforce the health and well-being of each student and staff member.
- School districts can use the WSCC model to guide collaborative efforts across administrators, staff, and community partners in different areas. As a result, schools can share new resources, ensure vertical alignment between grade levels to avoid duplication, and provide a consistent message to create awareness and gather support for the identified priority areas. Health education curricula and instruction should address the National Health Education Standards (NHES), so it's important to work with your physical education department of licensed teachers endorsed by the state to teach physical education based on the K-12 national standards.

In addition to the framework, I connected with other reputable organizations to learn about their resources and potential partnerships, and met with members of their staff to gather input as well.

Another important fact to note is, according to Debra Eschmeyer, executive director of Let's Move! and senior policy advisor for nutrition, "Over the past three decades, childhood obesity rates in America have tripled, and today, nearly one in three children in America are overweight or obese. The numbers are even higher in African American and Hispanic communities, where nearly 40 percent of the children are overweight or obese. If we don't solve this problem, one third of all children born in 2000 or later will suffer from diabetes at some point in their lives. Many others will face chronic obesity-related health problems like heart disease, high blood pressure, cancer, and asthma."

As teachers, our job is to be actively involved as healthy role models to potentially make a difference in reducing childhood obesity, and to make a positive difference in long-term health outcomes. Think about how many students' and families' lives we could positively affect each year. It's time to raise the bar in your school and community.

> *While budgets are tight right now, there are schools across the country that are showing that it doesn't take a whole lot of money or resources to give our kids the nutrition they deserve. What it does take, however, is effort. What it does take is imagination. What it does take is a commitment to our children's futures.*
>
> **—Michelle Obama**

As you talk with your administration, you might find the following talking points helpful.

- Academic achievement and health are closely linked. Let's provide more opportunities for health and wellness on campus and in classrooms for both the staff and students. Here are some ideas on how to do that:

- Let's form a wellness committee on site to self-assess our needs and form an action plan. (This is required for schools participating in NSLP, the federal school lunch program.) The PE teachers, administrators, nurse, school psychologist, etc. could . . .
- Let's use a variety of low-cost and free tools and frameworks, such as the Whole School, Whole Community, Whole Child (WSCC) Framework.
- Let's get the EduNinja on campus to lead professional development, which includes nutrition, movement, and mindfulness breakout sessions.
- Let's form a staff book club by reading *The EduNinja Mindset* and other nutrition, movement, and mindfulness material. This will help teachers better meet the needs of all learners; in addition, modeling these behaviors may possibly reduce sick days taken by staff or reduce the burnout rate.
- Let's get teachers in our schools to join a physical or online health and wellness community to extend their learning. Leverage the power of social media for our PLN. Connecting at eduninja.net for the #EduNinja 30-Day Health and Wellness Challenge is one option.
- Let's get community members and organizations committed to health and wellness involved in helping the students, families, and staff at our school. Some possible ones may be . . .

Forming a Health and Wellness Team

Think of the positive impact a nutrition, movement, and mindfulness focus at your school could have on your community. Start by bringing together a talented, passionate team to assess the needs of your school by using resources from eduninja.net or another organization to create an action plan. Sending out a health and wellness survey will help align the needs and goals for the action plan. The team can be administrators, PE teachers, school nurses, coaches, interested teachers, parents, etc.

You need champions within district buildings to sustain the work, replicate it, and drive positive change within your system to create widespread practices within the district. The PE teachers or individual teacher leaders in their classrooms aren't enough. Shared ownership is needed, and all voices need to be heard—from the school board, superintendent, teachers, and staff, to students, families, community businesses and organizations.

Getting Everyone Involved

Once you have a wellness team and a plan, principals need to embrace this work with schoolwide planned health and wellness opportunities throughout the year involving teachers, students, families, and community partners. This could involve whole school assemblies, schoolwide fitness days, implementing a school gardening program, or starting healthy lunch clubs or a healthier lunch program.

Teachers need to model and offer positive leadership to students daily by integrating nutrition, movement, and mindfulness within the classroom to fit the standards. As noted earlier, these can be scheduled into your lesson plans as a transition break, a stand-alone lesson, or integrated as a theme in a reading or writing block. And remember to offer strategies as you confer with students.

Health and wellness opportunities can range from offering activity-based afterschool programs, to providing teacher training for incorporating nutrition, movement, and mindfulness in the classroom, to gathering schoolwide speakers for children, teachers, and families, to leading fundraising events promoting health and wellness. Are there local businesses, schools, or nonprofit organizations you can partner with to promote nutrition, movement, or mindfulness?

You'll be surprised at the outpouring of people who may be able to help if you just have the courage to mention your mission. According to Norris Superintendent Dr. John Skretta, "Most people want to be enlisted in projects that transcend their own circumstances and expand their sphere of influence." Don't be afraid to call individuals or companies. Some may not be able to help, but they may lead you to others to help instill a healthier school environment for students, teachers, and families.

Connecting Globally to the Social Media Community

If you haven't connected with teachers on social media yet, now's your time. It's been one of my favorite ways to connect with innovative teachers to share ideas, collaborate on projects, learn about new technologies available, and see strategies teachers are successfully using in their classrooms. During the past two years while recovering from my Achilles tear, I've discovered that even though I was physically immobile, I was still able to mobilize and connect with people virtually. Don't let the size or location of your school or teaching philosophies within your district be an obstacle. Connect globally to find teachers within this community who believe in the importance of health and wellness as a strong foundation to all other goal setting and passions you have as an educator.

One way to connect to the global community of learners is by joining the #eduninja30 30-Day Health and Wellness Challenge. It's a great way to meet new friends while getting the staff at your school involved. Your family and friends will all be practicing healthy habits together.

An EduNinja Embodies Grit

Flex Your EduNinja Muscles

★ What healthy attributes and strategies can you bring from other positive communities to merge with your school to make it a happier, healthier, more engaging place for everyone to do their best teaching and learning?

★ What can you do to help your administration see the importance and benefits of forming a health and wellness committee? If your school already has a committee, then what can you do to help elevate its range, impact, and consistency with resources, standards alignment, and staff training?

★ How can you easily start adding teacher fitness to your weekly routine on or off campus with others?

★ What accountability strategies can you put into place to maintain teacher fitness consistency to see and feel the benefits?

★ How can you help build a healthy community between students, staff, families, and local organizations?

An EduNinja
Leaves a Legacy

*Everyone, everyone is a teacher. Everyone is a teacher
to someone; maybe it's your children, maybe it's a
neighbor, maybe it's someone under your
supervision in some other way, and in one way
or another, you're teaching them by your actions.*

—John Wooden

*No written word
No spoken plea
Can teach our youth what they should be.
Nor all the books on all the shelves,
It's what the teachers are themselves.*

—Anonymous

ohn Wooden believed that "Profound responsibilities come with teaching and coaching. You can do so much good—or harm. It's why I believe that next to parenting, teaching and coaching are the two most important professions in the world." We have all had a teacher or mentor in our life who's made a direct positive impact by helping us get to where we are today. We're grateful for these special individuals who shared important life messages we needed to learn and share with others. These people left us a legacy—they've helped us realize we're all teachers and learners and have taught us lessons we can pass on to our own students.

I'm forever grateful for Coach Rose. He believed in me from the start. He saw me—all five-foot-two of me with no big club volleyball experience—as a small setter who would eventually play as a defensive specialist on the Penn State Women's Volleyball Team. But most importantly, he saw me succeeding as a student athlete, something no one else had seen in me before.

Thanks to Coach Rose's belief in me, I earned Academic All-Big Ten Honors every single year at Penn State. This coach, teacher, and leader held me to high standards and pushed me every day. He set the highest bar for academic and athletic performance and somehow got me, a struggling high school student who didn't know how to play volleyball well, to become a defensive specialist and a graduate from Penn State University. My highest honor would be to become the type of teacher for my students Coach Rose was for me. I want my students to dream big, work hard, and have fun, while implementing strategies to be the best they can be in and out of the classroom.

Help Others Write Their Stories

Think back to when someone scripted you in a positive way or believed in you when you didn't think you could do something. They helped you write your story. I couldn't have written this particular story without the help from some of my major life influencers. We all have these influencers who have left us a legacy. Now it's our turn to be like them for someone else. You have the power to inspire someone because you believe in them. You listen to them, empathize with them, and encourage them to keep going.

Words like those of middle school principal Sean Gaillard, "This is your year," and Coach Rose, "Do what you do best, kid: fly high and free," have such power to show students we believe in them—and believe they can achieve great things. Our positive words can become a self-fulfilling prophecy for them, so encourage them to go beyond what they thought was possible.

Peg Pennepacker, my high school P.E. teacher, coach, and current founder of High School Title IX Services, LLC, reminds me that we need to encourage all students to pursue what they love and help them believe in being strong and true to themselves. We must take little steps in order to open doors for the young people who follow us since we are servant leaders in education.

I want to show my students I believe in them no matter what. I want to model dogged determination so my students can see how struggle can lead to success, and I want to keep pushing them to reach their success, no matter how long it takes. These are all invaluable life lessons I learned from Coach Rose, and I want to pass them on to my students. I didn't always learn quickly, but I'm still using the same lessons now to elevate and set bigger goals. Coach took a chance with me, and I'm grateful he did. He saw things in me I didn't think were possible. That's what makes him a great teacher. Coach John Wooden, the famous UCLA men's basketball coach, once said, "A good coach can change a game. A great coach can change a *life*." I know he was talking about Coach Russ Rose.

Leaving a Legacy for Diverse Learners

When I think about the legacy I want to leave, I think about my professional mission statement:

Building the foundation of sound nutrition, movement, and mindfulness to meet the needs of the teachers, students, and families.

But wrapped inside my mission is an added passion for students with diverse learning styles. Dyslexia provided me with an acute awareness of, and a passionate empathy for, diverse learners. My experiences helped form my mindset and enlightened my teaching with an appreciation of each person's inner genius. This has become my cornerstone to true teaching and a way to motivate our community of learners. I've learned if I want exceptional effort from my students, I have to show them they're valued and model how learning takes place in all its unique forms as it morphs, transpires, and inspires in many ways, both in and out of the classroom. Before high school, as a quiet student who didn't fit in to a system, I was overlooked and under-supported. I wasn't taught strategies for better learning, and I didn't have an academic support group to lean on. If I had learned mindfulness or social emotional tools, at the very least I would have had strategies to help with my self-worth and processing of emotions. But I had none of these things, leaving me holding on to everything internally and having no idea how to cope or get past these obstacles. By the time I reached high school, my needs had been neglected for so long, I'm sure my teachers and coaches didn't know how to help or how significant my learning challenges were.

Meeting the needs of all learners is always at the forefront of my mind when planning lessons: from the videos or audio being used, to the range of text levels, graphic organizers, manipulative tools, kinesthetic strategies, or other scaffolds students may need to best understand the information, push their thinking, and creatively show their learning. Small, flexible, heterogeneous and homogeneous groups, partner work, and daily conferring happens across all subjects. A strong reflection and refinement practice for teaching helps us to elevate and make our lessons better for all students to practice the EduNinja mindset.

As educators, we have to ensure all students are supported. We have to allow for wait time, turn and talk opportunities, and individual conferring times to allow everyone an equal voice. We have to build sharing opportunities into whole group lessons and small group sessions and include kinesthetic lessons. Through my own classroom, and now in sharing my story, I hope to help more students who are dealing with learning challenges.

Connect with Your Students

As educator Rita Pierson said so well in her TED Talk, "Kids can't learn from teachers they don't like." We know many students will work harder for their teachers who are rooting for them to succeed. Don't miss opportunities to connect with students during transition times and brain breaks to show you care. Dance with them, jump with them, and do push-ups with them. They'll appreciate you for it. If those things are out of your comfort zone, do them anyway. Otherwise, your students will notice and may be more apt to follow your lead and be less engaged in lessons throughout the day.

Having connection with your students allows you to have more opportunity to positively impact them. Seeing students who face similar obstacles to ones you've faced allows you to help them realize how lucky they are to think differently. You can provide them with positive encouragement and academic support and give them opportunity to engage their passions and creatively share their learning. You're able to hold students to high expectations, helping them believe they can achieve.

Connecting with your students will also make *you* a better teacher. I know my "Little Ninjas" push me to become a better teacher. I appreciate them because they inspire me to learn more about the best research-based teaching practices and technology, as well as finding new apps, creating new engaging lessons, and connecting on social media with other educators.

Flex Your EduNinja Muscles

★ Who are your significant mentors? Have you told them how they've impacted your life? (If not, I challenge you to write them a thank you note, email or text, or meet them for lunch.) How are you living your life to make your mentors proud? What would they do in any tough situation?

★ What do you do to show your students you believe in them no matter what? How do you keep pushing students to succeed no matter how long it takes?

★ How are you meeting the needs of all types of learners? How are students given opportunities to show their learning in different ways?

★ What legacy do you want to leave for your students?

Final Thoughts
on Becoming
an EduNinja

The "12" is the chapter number within the star graphic.

*Champions aren't made in gyms. Champions
are made from something they have deep
inside them—a desire, a dream, a vision.*

—Muhammad Ali

*Success is peace of mind, which is a direct result
of self-satisfaction in knowing you did your best to
become the best that you are capable of becoming.*

—John Wooden

I almost said it was too much—I couldn't do it. But as I was writing this book, the process literally changed my own mindset. I knew it was time to raise my own bar. I knew I could teach full-time at a high-performing district, lead with a health and wellness team, speak at schools, lead professional development for teachers at conferences, participate in teacher vodcasts, lead and join Twitter chats, teach EduNinja™ Fit classes, write this book, lead EduNinja™ Fit field trips for families, start the EduNinja™ nonprofit organization to educate students in underserved areas about the importance of nutrition, movement, and mindfulness, *and* do my own training for obstacle racing—all while spending quality time with the people I love.

Ironically, the reflective process involved in writing this book gave me added energy even though I was doing more. I was looking back on my trials and failures, the ups and the downs. I was maintaining positive vision while staying grounded in the present moment. I was practicing journaling, positive affirmations, elevated goals, greener nutrition, and drinking more water. Plus, I was surrounding myself with awesome people, doing more of what I love, being mindful, and sharing my new learning with even more people.

I had a renewed vision of what truly was possible. I started saying "yes" to more opportunities, learning more, experiencing more, giving more, and not letting any limiting ideas cloud my vision. I was easily able to hop on a red-eye flight to catch the train in order to meet amazing educational influencers at a principal's conference for breakfast. Afterward I spent time with my nieces, got work done, then ran up a mountain full of obstacles with friends before flying home. I returned home refocused on training, writing, getting the EduNinja™ nonprofit dialed in, and preparing my keynote speeches. I felt elevated and empowered.

With the school year starting in just a few weeks, my publishing date approaching, and a keynote presentation to prepare, I was asked by some amazing athletes to run in an upcoming team race. The old me would have said, "No way." With so much on my plate, I'd never be able to train enough to compete at that level. A few weeks ago, I wouldn't have thought it was possible to operate at a high level in all areas. Surprisingly, it now seemed manageable. What changed? My mindset. I had raised the bar. I had started saying "yes" without worrying about perfection.

This is where the "ninja" part of EduNinja kicks in. You start saying "yes" and seeing the possibilities. You start finding different ways to get things done more effectively. Ninjas are flexible thinkers, problem-solvers, and creative. If they miss a step, they just keep going. They never give up looking for new ways and opportunities to get the job done and have fun.

It's Your Turn

Turn on your EduNinja mindset. Have the courage to say "yes" to something you usually wouldn't do, knowing people want to support you. Meet with and be inspired by them. Sometimes you need other people's perspectives to help you see the possibilities you didn't think were there. Step into your community, and step up to elevated, empowering opportunities. Set the bar higher and be amazed by what you can do.

For me, *American Ninja Warrior* was a transformative process from the inside out. I now believe I have the potential to overcome any obstacle with hard work and dedication. I face my own insecurities and develop courage to attempt seemingly impossible obstacles, maintaining determination and persistence to keep going when things get difficult. I'm a teacher, but I will forever be a student—learning, growing, and refining.

I'm a teacher, but I will forever be a student—learning, growing, and refining.

As you size up the obstacles in the school year, you know there's pressure from parents, administrators, coaches, and stakeholders for students to meet their growth targets. At first glance, it's easy to get overwhelmed with the challenges you'll face: learning new curriculum, using new technology, communicating with parents, the occasional lice outbreak, student disagreements from foursquare making their way back to the classroom, and keeping students motivated and engaged in learning. Your life-work balance will be tested, as will your agility, flexibility of thinking, positive mindset, physical strength, mental fortitude, stamina, willpower, and perseverance to successfully finish the obstacle course—I mean "school year." It's easy to think, "How am I going to get through this?"

The answer? Turn on the EduNinja mindset.

This is the same mindset I use when running an obstacle course, working out in the gym—*and* when looking at the school year. The EduNinja mindset is overcoming the fear of failure, knowing it takes courage to set goals with soul. It's being okay with lots of trying, failing, reflecting, refining, repeating daily effort using different strategies, celebrating micro gains, and showing grit by not quitting when things get tough or frustrating. It's pushing the accelerator at the exact moment when you want to quit. It's looking at failure as opportunity and having the will and determination to finish what you set out to do. It's trusting the process—developing the skills necessary to eventually become successful.

EduNinjas are experts at constantly practicing balance. Whether it's on the obstacle course or in life, they know the importance of slowing down to purposefully enjoy the true moments unfolding minute to minute. These high achievers can also be spotted fully focused and enjoying the practice of overcoming extreme feats, sparked by a strong intrinsic motivation to achieve personal greatness. (That's why you are reading this book right now.)

EduNinjas know their personal responsibility is to push themselves, keep going, embrace the uncomfortable with positivity, and succeed. They know failure leads to learning opportunities and are intrinsically rewarded for working at their personal best. They possess a growth mindset, knowing learning never ends.

EduNinjas dream big and visualize their goals, knowing it takes continual practice to fully visualize the end goal while staying grounded and disciplined in every step of the journey. They embrace all the ups, downs, and sideways places they find themselves. They talk about their goals, dreams, successes, and setbacks in terms of *when* they'll achieve them, not *if* they'll achieve them, knowing if they aren't succeeding yet, they will eventually overcome any obstacle in their path and attract the right community of individuals to help them succeed. EduNinjas never give up.

We're all here to support one another as we continually raise the bar to practice these mind-body connection strategies. Together we will keep learning, grinding, and writing our own magnificent stories. Use the hashtag #BestSchoolYearYet to share these elevating and empowering strategies, and encourage your students, coworkers, and family to do the same.

I wish you the very best school year yet, and I can't wait to see everyone for the #eduninja30 30-Day Health and Wellness Challenge!

Flex Your EduNinja Muscles

★ What does daily success look like to you in your *personal life*? What day-to-day obstacles are holding you back? How could you use your EduNinja mindset to overcome these personal obstacles?

★ What does daily success look like to you in your *professional life*? What day-to-day obstacles are holding you back? How could you use your EduNinja mindset to overcome these professional obstacles?

★ What does success look like to you in your *classroom for students*? What day-to-day obstacles are holding you back? How could you use your EduNinja mindset to overcome these classroom obstacles?

Appendix

Nutrition Tips to Feel Fueled and Ready to Teach

Highlight one or two a week you want to focus on. Each week or two, add in another tip.

★ Don't go on a diet. Instead, be mindful when you make your grocery list and when you decide where you shop, what you choose to take home, the portion sizes you eat, and when you eat. Consistently keep exercising.

★ When grocery shopping, only buy items that will spoil, shop the perimeter for the healthy items, and try shopping at smaller, healthier stores.

★ Buy in-season vegetables for maximum flavor at a lower cost. Check your local market for the best in-season buys or visit your local farmers market.

★ Make half your plate vegetables and complement with protein and complex carbs, and maybe eat a serving of fruit or a small almond milk smoothie as dessert. Be mindful of serving sizes.

★ Remember that you are eating food because it fuels your body, not just because it tastes good.

★ Try reducing your sugar by reading nutrition labels. Men only need nine teaspoons a day, and women only need six.

★ Use healthy herbs and spices, such as cinnamon, chili peppers, turmeric, garlic, oregano, parsley, basil, thyme, and rosemary.

★ Try cooking foods with red or green chili pepper to help boost your metabolic rate temporarily.

★ If you go out to eat, split a meal with a friend or ask for half of your meal to be boxed up for tomorrow's lunch before it comes to the table.

★ Reward and comfort students with attention and care, not treats. Rewarding children with sweet desserts or snacks may encourage them to think treats are better than other foods.

★ Consume small amounts of unsaturated fat from nuts and olive oil. For omega-3 fats, eat fatty fish like salmon.

★ Prep daily meals on Sunday by assembling food healthy in quality and quantity, using reusable containers.

★ Limit caffeine and try choosing green tea instead of coffee. Green tea contains antioxidants to fight, and possibly prevent, cell damage. A range of research shows green tea benefits the heart and brain.

★ Start the day with a green smoothie or low-sugar oatmeal.

★ Buy low-sodium soup broth and make soup as a quick lunch at school. Add quinoa, fresh herbs, vegetables, and protein.

★ Eat healthy carbs such as whole grains, beans, fruits, and vegetables. Healthy carbs are digested slowly, helping you feel full longer and keeping blood sugar and insulin levels stable.

★ Avoid refined carbs such as breads, pastas, and non-whole-grain cereals. Unhealthy carbs are foods such as white flour, refined sugar, and white rice and have been stripped of all bran, fiber, and nutrients. They digest quickly and cause spikes in blood sugar levels and energy.

★ Power up with proteins such as pea protein, quinoa, beans, egg whites, hummus, and possibly salmon, lean turkey, or white chicken.

★ Don't skip meals. Eat smaller portions every three to four hours.

★ Eat fresh fruit instead of drinking fruit juice to get the benefits of the fiber.

★ Prepare as many meals at home as possible, where you can easily control the ingredients, portion sizes, and nutritional value.

★ Stay hydrated by setting an hourly alarm on your phone (or having a student ring a water bell) to drink a cup of water every hour. Choose water over sugary drinks. Consume plenty of water before, during, and after exercising.

★ Limit traditional desserts or share with a friend.

★ Skip the bread or tortilla and make lettuce wraps instead for lunch.

★ Eat naturally sweet vegetables, such as sweet potatoes and yams, in moderation. They add healthy sweetness to your meals and may reduce your cravings for added sugars.

However, they do add sugar so be mindful of portion sizes. They still have a lower glycemic index than white potatoes.

★ Start a home or school garden.

★ When buying or building a smoothie at home, notice how much sugar is in the juice and frozen fruit. Calories add up quickly.

★ Take care of gut health with probiotics. If you drink kombucha to promote good gut health, be mindful of the sugar.

★ Snack on small amounts of unsalted nuts like almonds to help curb your appetite. One serving size is about ten almonds.

★ Eat black beans, garbanzo beans, and black-eyed peas for a low fat, inexpensive, fiber-packed protein source (21 percent protein). Try adding ¼ cup to meals as an alternative source of protein.

★ Slow down and eat mindfully. Don't multitask. Eat with others. Be mindful enough to stop eating before you feel full since it actually takes a few minutes for your brain to tell your body it has had enough food.

★ Use a food journal. Focus on how you feel after you've been eating healthy regularly. Do you have fewer up and down spikes? Feel less guilty? Have more energy overall?

Ideas for Kinesthetic Activities

Create opportunities for students to express themselves through movement, hands-on activities, and the opportunity to manipulate materials. Try adding these activities to your lessons or units of study.

★ Design a game.

★ Create a newsletter.

★ Write a letter.

★ Design a brochure.

★ Make a diorama.

★ Organize an event or activity.

★ Investigate how something works.

★ Make a clay model.

★ Do a volunteer project.

★ Make visual aids for a presentation.

★ Make a storyboard and practice storytelling.

★ Give a speech.

★ Perform a skit.

★ Construct a model.

★ Paint, draw, sketch, etc.

★ Perform a dance.

★ Create lyrics and sing.

★ Take photos.

★ Plan a campaign for a cause or issue.

★ Make a video.

★ Perform music.

★ Do choral reading.

★ Create a cartoon.

★ Do an experiment.

★ Participate in a debate.

★ Make a poster.

★ Develop an invention.

★ Conduct an interview.

★ Role-play.

★ Solve problems.

The EduNinja 30-Day Challenge

The EduNinja 30-Day Health and Wellness Challenge was created to meet the needs of all educators at any fitness level to help build community, support each other in trying new physical activities, learn about healthy food choices, incorporate kinesthetic lessons and brain breaks into the classroom, and experience positive benefits to carry over into all parts of life.

My passionate lifelong dedication to sports training urged me to see how I could help teachers learn more about health and wellness while experiencing the benefits of connecting and helping one another achieve better health and fitness goals with a differentiated challenge. With almost twenty years of teaching experience, I knew many teachers were looking for strategies for battling fatigue, stress, and poor diets acquired by trying to feel better and deal with the stress of teaching. It was a vicious cycle. I knew there were solutions and knew I'd be able to help.

Building relationships within this EduNinja 30-Day Challenge community is the most important goal. Knowing others care helps tremendously to live up to both personal goals and expectations of the group's norms, helping ourselves while getting and giving support. Teachers, staff members, administrators, and families all have opportunities to meet new friends in this supportive group. Many are educators, from all over the country, who are joining together no matter their current fitness level.

One person's goal might be to walk on all days of the challenge while progressively increasing steps, another person's goal may be to get her whole school involved in the EduNinja 30-Day Challenge, while another person may want to do every exercise every day of the challenge. Everyone in the group is encouraged to share his or her daily movement with the group where it's celebrated. Taking daily, measurable steps to achieve individual goals and getting healthier from whatever point individuals are starting from, while having the support of peers, is the goal. When teachers are practicing healthier habits and connecting with a supportive group, they are happier, less stressed, and better teachers for their students.

Sample Letter to Get Others Involved

This is the letter I posted at eduninja.net to help other teachers, staff, administrators, and families understand the purpose of the EduNinja 30-Day Health and Wellness Challenge and how they can help spread the word and build community. You could send a group text or an email with the eduninja.net link to a group of people who you think would love this or benefit from this health challenge. Wouldn't everyone benefit? Principals would benefit from having a healthier and happier staff. Coworkers would have positive opportunities to connect with one another. Students would have a more engaging teacher, and students could participate at their individual level along with their families at home as well. Together we can make a difference in creating healthier, happier schools where better learning can take place.

Hello Teachers, Administrators, School Staff, and Friends,

My name is Jennifer Burdis. You may know me as the EduNinja™. I am a twenty-year veteran elementary teacher, keynote speaker, NSCA-Certified Personal Trainer, and author. I grew up in Pennsylvania, and sports were an important part of my life, from playing volleyball at Penn State to competing on NBC's *American Ninja Warrior* seasons six and seven.

With my first book coming out in June titled *The EduNinja Mindset: 11 Habits for Building a Stronger Mind and Body*, I'm excited to share with all people, especially teachers, administrators, and school staff the importance of giving yourself the gift of health and wellness to better serve others. When you feel better, you may teach better, and students can potentially learn better from teachers who are healthy, happy, and engaged in their lessons.

May 17–June 15 marks the third annual EduNinja 30-Day Challenge. #eduninja30 will again inspire educators to incorporate physical activity, healthy eating, kinesthetic lessons, and mindfulness into the classroom promoting a culture of health in schools while building community across the nation. Please join teachers, families, and friends who are giving themselves the gift of health and wellness this month.

The easiest way to join this health and wellness party and stay connected with your EduFriends is to tell your principal, tell your friends on social media, and ask your coworkers to join you. We're going to be moving some desks out of the way, or you may end up working out in your pj's before school because these EduNinja workouts can be completed just about anywhere! These workouts are adapted for all levels, and you can try as many new exercises by looking at the easy-to-follow weekly videos on eduninja.net under the #eduninja30 tab.

Please be sure to consult your physician before starting any workout program. I encourage you to talk to your healthcare provider today to learn about your blood pressure, cholesterol, blood sugar, BMI (Body Mass Index) and any prior health conditions or injuries. It is also recommended to have a certified personal trainer help you determine what level to start at, if appropriate, and help guide you with proper form through these exercises.

There are so many ways you can participate. Choose your favorite social media tool to stay connected.

What You'll Need Before You Start

★ Sign up at: eduninja.net.

★ Request access to the private "eduninja30" Facebook group where we support, encourage, and build community with awesome teachers, administrators, and friends.

★ Follow and tag @jennifer_burdis on Twitter with #eduninja30, follow eduninja30 or jenniferburdis on Instagram.

★ Please help spread the word among other teachers, staff, and administrators. Don't forget to use the #eduninja30 when you post pictures.

It might be helpful to prepare by doing the following:

- ★ Purchase a yoga mat.
- ★ Download the Tabata Pro app.
- ★ Obtain a Swiss Ball and medicine ball (purchase, borrow these, or get access to a gym with them).

Preparing for the Challenge

Have a forty-ounce reusable water container at your desk and have students keep a reusable water container at their desks too. Have a student ring a water bell every hour and have everyone drink out of their water container. Try finishing the forty ounces before the end of the school day.

Log your meals and beverages daily. Try adding more vegetables, while still eating high quality proteins, and complex carbs. Be mindful of portion sizes and reducing foods that contain sugar, salt, and saturated fats. Try buying almost all perishable foods and get in the habit of eating an earlier dinner—not right before bedtime.

Commit to going to bed before 10:00 p.m., knowing you'll feel better in the morning. Sleep plays a huge part in your willpower when it comes to choosing to exercise and eating well.

Gather a group of fun teachers and decide on a place to meet to do the daily workouts together before, during (with administration approval during school lunch hours, of course), or after school.

The Fitness Part of the EduNinja 30-Day Challenge

Week 1

Level 1: 20-25 minutes of cardio such as: walking, biking, stair stepper, etc. 2-3 x a week.

Level 2: 30-35 minutes of cardio such as: hiking, jogging, biking, stair stepper, etc. 4-5 x a week.

Level 3: 45-50 minutes of cardio such as: jogging, biking, stair stepper, etc. 5-6 x a week.

Post a picture with #eduninja30 on social media or in the private "eduninja30" Facebook group.

Week 2

Level 1: 25-30 minutes of cardio such as: walking, biking, stair stepper, etc. 2-3 x a week.

Level 2: 35-40 minutes of cardio such as: hiking, jogging, biking, stair stepper, etc. 4-5 x a week.

Level 3: 55-60 minutes of cardio such as: jogging, biking, stair stepper, etc. 5-6 x a week.

Post a picture with #eduninja30 on social media or in the private "eduninja30" Facebook group.

Week 3

Level 1: 25-30+ minutes of cardio such as: brisk walking, biking, stair stepper, etc. 2-3 x a week.

Level 2: 35-45+ minutes of cardio such as: hiking, jogging, biking, stair stepper, etc. 4-5 x a week.

Level 3: 55-60+ minutes of cardio such as: jogging, biking, stair stepper, etc. 5-6 x a week.

Post a picture with #eduninja30 on social media or in the private "eduninja30" Facebook group.

Week 4

Level 1: 30+ minutes of cardio such as: brisk walking, biking, stair stepper, etc. 3 x a week.

Level 2: 45+ minutes of cardio such as: hiking, jogging, biking, stair stepper, etc. 5 x a week.

Level 3: 60+ minutes of cardio such as: jogging, biking, stair stepper, etc. 6 x a week.

Post a picture with #eduninja30 on social media or in the private "eduninja30" Facebook group to inspire others.

Each week I'll post one video sharing four exercises to add to your cardio routine. Please download the Tabata Pro Timer.

Level 1: Stay committed to your fun movement goals. Could you try one new exercise from the EduNinja Challenge weekly video?

Level 2: Could you add 1-2 sets of the EduNinja Challenge weekly exercises to your cardio days?

Level 3: Could you add 2-3 sets of the EduNinja Challenge weekly exercises added to your cardio days?

If you are looking for a way to hold yourself more account-
able in reaching your goals, getting the daily workout, trying
new brain breaks, gathering kinesthetic lesson ideas, getting
nutrition and mindfulness tools, and making better daily
food choices, then please join us on Facebook at eduninja30.
We're better together, so let's do this! Together we can inspire
healthy students, teachers, principals, and superintendents
across the country.

Twitter: jennifer_burdis
Facebook: "eduninja30" private group (ask to join)
Instagram: eduninja30 or jenniferburdis
Website: eduninja.net

What a great way to kickoff summer!

Sincerely,

Jen Burdis

Acknowledgments

I wouldn't be where I am today without . . .

* My **mom** and **dad**, for their love and guidance. They know when I get a passionate project opportunity I give it my all. **Dad,** you showed me the importance of hard work and not taking myself so seriously; **Mom**, I appreciate the endless sacrifices you made for our family and your continued support.

* My brother **Neil**, who taught me how to keep competing, having fun, and enjoying life's daily gifts; My brother **Tim** who continually shows me maturity beyond his years that I aspire to. Thanks to you both, along with Jackie and Michele, for enriching my days and sharing the daily joys of my awesome little nieces.

* **Mr. Kulich,** who taught me how science and learning can be as fun as the volleyball and basketball he coached.

* **Coach Rose,** who helped develop the EduNinja Mindset in a pint-sized athlete and elementary reader, encouraged me to play Division 1 volleyball, and expected me not just to get a college education, but to achieve academic awards.

* **John Skretta**, a huge health and wellness catalyst and inspiration, who gave me my first keynote speech

opportunity in front of an auditorium of teachers, and encouraged me to write this book.

★ **Sean Gaillard,** who believed in the idea of *The EduNinja Mindset* from the very beginning and provided constant positive leadership and inspiration.

★ **Matt Stankiewitch,** for handing me a copy of *The Alchemist* to help me connect my passion and purpose.

★ **Adam Taliaferro,** who helped me gain perspective about injuries and coming out stronger.

★ The entire Penn State Volleyball sisterhood of empowering teammates and life-long friends; **Teri,** for suggesting I should try out for *American Ninja Warrior*; **Angie,** for helping me pinpoint my vision of helping others reach for their personal "greatness."

★ My family of ninjas, especially **Cory**, **Steve**, and **James**, who keep me grounded, connected, and grateful to be a ninja.

★ **The Sanns**, who always treat me like family with their kindness.

★ **Peg Pennepacker,** who reminds me to encourage all students to pursue what they love.

★ **Stacey Halboth,** for sharing mindfulness strategies with her friends and her students. Thanks for always believing in me.

★ The awesome fourth grade team of teachers, **Jen Overstreet, Mandy Valentine, Haley Cameron,** and **Lexi Allred** who truly achieve more together. I'm grateful to work with you all.

- ★ The **entire staff at our school** for inspiring me with their hard work and kindness.

- ★ **Katrina Stainton** and **Julie Buechler** for being incredible "room moms" and keeping our classroom community of families connected this school year.

- ★ **Carole Kamery**, for being my number one hiking buddy.

- ★ **Our Garden Angel**, who helped plant our fourth-grade garden with kale, chard, and lettuce so we could taste the benefits of a healthy harvest in salads and smoothies.

- ★ **Dave and Shelley Burgess,** for believing a teacher who couldn't read or write well could craft a book to share information with others, and for their continued leadership in the teaching community.

- ★ **Tanya Baumgartner** and **Andrea Grillot,** who provided moral support to keep writing, despite my grammatical flaws.

- ★ **Erin Casey** and her team at My Writers' Connection, for helping me tell my story.

- ★ **Greg Ronlov,** for his photography skills and believing in this work.

- ★ **Shelly Cook** for creating a fun hair style to match the EduNinja Mindset.

- ★ **My "Little Ninjas," who push me to new heights with my learning and recess workouts.**

Without the help of these major life influencers, I couldn't have written this particular story.

If your organization is looking to build
a healthier culture, set bigger goals,
develop grit, enhance performance,
and strengthen relationships,

bring Jen Burdis to your team, school, or business!

Jen's custom-designed presentations will help your staff and students live with passion, persistence, and resilience. Some of her most popular presentations include . . .

★ *The EduNinja™ Mindset*
Educators will learn strategies for enhancing personal wellness and achievement while incorporating daily nutrition, movement, and mindfulness strategies in and out of the classroom.

★ *It's Time To Raise The Bar With EduNinja™ Nutrition, Movement, and Mindfulness*
This speech aims at empowering audience members to elevate their personal wellness using The EduNinja™ Mindset. Through reflective practices that reveal how obstacles can be turned into strengths, your team will learn skills that help them live stronger inside and out.

★ *It's Time To Raise The Bar With The EduNinja™ Mindset*

With a focus on setting and achieving ambitious life goals, this presentation equips educators and leaders with the tools to grow while inspiring their students, clients, and families. Jen will provide your team with foundational skills that empower, inspire, and engage them to realize their dreams and develop a mindset for success.

To learn more about developing the EduNinja Mindset in your school, home, and business, visit:

 eduninja.net

 Email Jen:
ninjajenburdis@gmail.com

Notes

Chapter 1:

Riordian, Rick. "An Interview with Rick." Rickriordian.com. rickriordan.com/about/an-interview-with-rick/ (accessed April 5, 2018).

Malcolm Gladwell. *David and Goliath: Underdogs, Misfits, and the Art of Battling Giants.* (New York: Hachette Book Group, 2013).

Chapter 8:

Kotz, Deborah and Haupt, Angela. "7 Mind-Blowing Benefits of Exercise." USNews.com. health.usnews.com/health-news/diet-fitness/slideshows/7-mind-blowing-benefits-of-exercise (accessed April 5, 2018)

American Heart Association. "For the Educator." heart.org/HEARTORG/Educator/Educator_UCM_001113_SubHomePage.jsp (accessed April 5, 2018)

John Ratey, MD's, Facebook page. Accessed April 15, 2018. facebook.com/JohnRateyMD/posts/10154410550084462

De La Cruz, Donna. "Why Kids Shouldn't Sit Still in Class." NYTimes.com. nytimes.com/2017/03/21/well/family/why-kids-shouldnt-sit-still-in-class.html (accessed April 5, 2018).

Chapter 9:

Kabat Zinn, Jon. "Mindful." Filmed May 2015. YouTube video, duration 2:08. Posted May 2015. easybib.com/guides/citation-guides/chicago-turabian/youtube-video/.

DeLlosa, Patty. "The Neurobiology of We." drdansiegel.com/
uploads/The%20Neurobiology%20of%20We%20-%20Patty%20
de%20Llosa.pdf.

Mindful Schools. "Evidence of the Benefits of Mindfulness
in Schools." MindfulSchools.org. mindfulschools.org/about-
mindfulness/research/#mindfulness-with-teachers (accessed
April 5, 2018).

Chapter 10:

Angela Duckworth, "Grit: The Power of Passion and
Perseverance." Filmed in April 2013. TED Video, 6:09. ted.com/
talks/angela_lee_duckworth_grit_the_power_of_passion_and_
perseverance.

Let's Move! "Learn the Facts." Let'sMove.gov. letsmove.
obamawhitehouse.archives.gov/learn-facts/epidemic-
childhood-obesity (Accessed April 5, 2018).

Holecko, Catherine. "First Lady Michelle Obama: Child Health
and Obesity Quotes." VeryWellFamily.com. verywellfamily.
com/michelle-obama-quotes-on-childhood-obesity-1257092
(accessed April 5, 2018)

Chapter 11:

Gallimore, Ronald. "No Spoken Plea Can Teach Our Youth What
They Should Be." Personal communication from John Wooden,
February 12, 2002. RonaldGallimore.com. ronaldgallimore.com/
styled/styled-12/index.html.

Rita Pierson, Every Kid Needs a Champion," May 2013, 7:45,
ted.com/talks/rita_pierson_every_kid_needs_a_champion.

More from

LEAD Like a PIRATE

Make School Amazing for Your Students and Staff

By Shelley Burgess and Beth Houf
(@Burgess_Shelley, @BethHouf)

Lead Like a PIRATE maps out character traits necessary to captain a school or district. You'll learn where to find treasure already in your classrooms and schools—and bring out the best in educators. Find encouragement in your relentless quest to make school amazing for everyone!

Lead with Culture

What Really Matters in Our Schools

By Jay Billy (@JayBilly2)

In this Lead Like a PIRATE Guide, Jay Billy explains that making school a place where students and staff want to be starts with culture. You'll be inspired by this principal's practical ideas for creating a sense of unity—even in the most diverse communities.

Teach Like a PIRATE

Increase Student Engagement, Boost Your Creativity, and Transform Your Life as an Educator

By Dave Burgess (@BurgessDave)

New York Times' bestseller *Teach Like a PIRATE* sparked a worldwide educational revolution with its passionate teaching manifesto and dynamic student-engagement strategies. Translated into multiple languages, it sparks outrageously creative lessons and life-changing student experiences.

Learn Like a PIRATE

Empower Your Students to Collaborate, Lead, and Succeed

By Paul Solarz (@PaulSolarz)

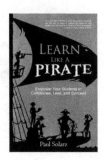

Passing grades don't equip students for life and career responsibilities. *Learn Like a PIRATE* shows how risk-taking and exploring passions in stimulating, motivating, supportive, self-directed classrooms create students capable of making smart, responsible decisions on their own.

P is for PIRATE

Inspirational ABC's for Educators

By Dave and Shelley Burgess (@Burgess_Shelley)

In *P is for Pirate,* husband-and-wife team Dave and Shelley Burgess tap personal experiences of seventy educators to inspire others to create fun and exciting places to learn. It's a wealth of imaginative and creative ideas that make learning and teaching more fulfilling than ever before.

eXPlore Like a Pirate

Gamification and Game-Inspired Course Design to Engage, Enrich, and Elevate Your Learners

By Michael Matera (@MrMatera)

Create an experiential, collaborative, and creative world with classroom game designer and educator Michael Matera's game-based learning book, *eXPlore Like a Pirate.* Matera helps teachers apply motivational gameplay techniques and enhance curriculum with gamification strategies.

Play Like a Pirate

Engage Students with Toys, Games, and Comics

By Quinn Rollins (@jedikermit)

In *Play Like a Pirate,* Quinn Rollins offers practical, engaging strategies and resources that make it easy to integrate fun into your curriculum. Regardless of grade level, serious learning can be seriously fun with inspirational ideas that engage students in unforgettable ways.

The Innovator's Mindset

Empower Learning, Unleash Talent, and Lead a Culture of Creativity

By George Couros (@gcouros)

In *The Innovator's Mindset*, teachers and administrators discover that compliance to a scheduled curriculum hinders student innovation, critical thinking, and creativity. To become forward-thinking leaders, students must be empowered to wonder and explore.

Pure Genius

Building a Culture of Innovation and Taking 20% Time to the Next Level

By Don Wettrick (@DonWettrick)

Collaboration—with experts, students, and other educators—helps create interesting and even life-changing opportunities for learning. In *Pure Genius*, Don Wettrick inspires and equips educators with a systematic blueprint for beating classroom boredom and teaching innovation.

Ditch That Textbook

Free Your Teaching and Revolutionize Your Classroom

By Matt Miller (@jmattmiller)

Ditch That Textbook creates a support system, toolbox, and manifesto that can free teachers from outdated textbooks. Miller empowers them to untether themselves, throw out meaningless, pedestrian teaching and learning practices, and evolve and revolutionize their classrooms.

50 Things You Can Do with Google Classroom

By Alice Keeler and Libbi Miller
(@alicekeeler, @MillerLibbi)

50 Things You Can Do with Google Classroom provides a thorough overview of this GAfE app and shortens the teacher learning curve for introducing technology in the classroom. Keeler and Miller's ideas, instruction, and screenshots help teachers go digital with this powerful tool.

50 Things to Go Further with Google Classroom

A Student-Centered Approach

By Alice Keeler and Libbi Miller
(@alicekeeler, @MillerLibbi)

In *50 Things to Go Further with Google Classroom: A Student-Centered Approach*, authors and educators Alice Keeler and Libbi Miller help teachers create a digitally rich, engaging, student-centered environment that taps the power of individualized learning using Google Classroom.

140 Twitter Tips for Educators

Get Connected, Grow Your Professional Learning Network, and Reinvigorate Your Career

By Brad Currie, Billy Krakower, and Scott Rocco
(@bradmcurrie, @wkrakower, @ScottRRocco)

In *140 Twitter Tips for Educators*, #Satchat hosts and founders of Evolving Educators, Brad Currie, Billy Krakower, and Scott Rocco, offer step-by-step instruction on Twitter basics and building an online following within Twitter's vibrant network of educational professionals.

Master the Media

How Teaching Media Literacy Can Save Our Plugged-In World

By Julie Smith (@julnilsmith)

Master the Media explains media history, purpose, and messaging, so teachers and parents can empower students with critical-thinking skills, which lead to informed choices, the ability to differentiate between truth and lies, and discern perception from reality. Media literacy can save the world.

The Zen Teacher

Creating Focus, Simplicity, and Tranquility in the Classroom

By Dan Tricarico (@thezenteacher)

Unrushed and fully focused, teachers influence—even improve—the future when they maximize performance and improve their quality of life. In *The Zen Teacher*, Dan Tricarico offers practical, easy-to-use techniques to develop a non-religious Zen practice and thrive in the classroom.

Your School Rocks . . . So Tell People!

Passionately Pitch and Promote the Positives Happening on Your Campus

By Ryan McLane and Eric Lowe (@McLane_Ryan, @EricLowe21)

Your School Rocks . . . So Tell People! helps schools create effective social media communication strategies that keep students' families and the community connected to what's going on at school, offering more than seventy immediately actionable tips with easy-to-follow instructions and video tutorial links.

The Classroom Chef

Sharpen Your Lessons. Season Your Classes. Make Math Meaningful

By John Stevens and Matt Vaudrey (@Jstevens009, @MrVaudrey)

With imagination and preparation, every teacher can be *The Classroom Chef* using John Stevens and Matt Vaudrey's secret recipes, ingredients, and tips that help students "get" math. Use ideas as-is, or tweak to create enticing educational meals that engage students.

How Much Water Do We Have?

5 Success Principles for Conquering Any Challenge and Thriving in Times of Change

By Pete Nunweiler with Kris Nunweiler

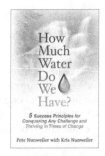

Stressed out, overwhelmed, or uncertain at work or home? It could be figurative dehydration.

How Much Water Do We Have? identifies five key elements necessary for success of any goal, life transition, or challenge. Learn to find, acquire, and use the 5 Waters of Success.

The Writing on the Classroom Wall

How Posting Your Most Passionate Beliefs about Education Can Empower Your Students, Propel Your Growth, and Lead to a Lifetime of Learning

By Steve Wyborney (@SteveWyborney)

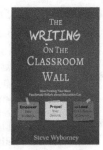

Big ideas lead to deeper learning, but they don't have to be profound to have profound impact. Teacher Steve Wyborney explains why and how sharing ideas sharpens and refines them. It's okay if some ideas fall off the wall; what matters most is sharing and discussing.

Kids Deserve It!

Pushing Boundaries and Challenging Conventional Thinking

By Todd Nesloney and Adam Welcome
(@TechNinjaTodd, @awelcome)

   Think big. Make learning fun and meaningful. *Kids Deserve It!* Nesloney and Welcome offer high-tech, high-touch, and highly engaging practices that inspire risk-taking and shake up the status quo on behalf of your students. Rediscover why you became an educator, too!

LAUNCH

Using Design Thinking to Boost Creativity and Bring Out the Maker in Every Student

By John Spencer and A.J. Juliani (@spencerideas, @ajjuliani)

   When students identify themselves as makers, inventors, and creators, they discover powerful problem-solving and critical-thinking skills. Their imaginations and creativity will shape our future. John Spencer and A.J. Juliani's *LAUNCH* process dares you to innovate and empower them.

Instant Relevance

Using Today's Experiences to Teach Tomorrow's Lessons

By Denis Sheeran (@MathDenisNJ)

   Learning sticks when it's relevant to students. In *Instant Relevance,* author and keynote speaker Denis Sheeran equips you to create engaging lessons *from* experiences and events that matter to students while helping them make meaningful connections between the real world and the classroom.

Escaping the School Leader's Dunk Tank

How to Prevail When Others Want to See You Drown

By Rebecca Coda and Rick Jetter
(@RebeccaCoda, @RickJetter)

   Dunk-tank situations—discrimination, bad politics, revenge, or ego-driven coworkers—can make an educator's life miserable. Coda and Jetter (dunk-tank survivors themselves) share real-life stories and insightful research to equip school leaders with tools to survive and, better yet, avoid getting "dunked."

Start. Right. Now.

Teach and Lead for Excellence

By Todd Whitaker, Jeff Zoul, and Jimmy Casas
(@ToddWhitaker, @Jeff_Zoul, @casas_jimmy)

Excellent leaders and teachers *Know the Way, Show the Way, Go the Way, and Grow Each Day*. Whitaker, Zoul, and Casas share four key behaviors of excellence from educators across the U.S. and motivate to put you on the right path.

Teaching Math with Google Apps

50 G Suite Activities

By Alice Keeler and Diana Herrington

(@AliceKeeler, @mathdiana)

Teaching Math with Google Apps meshes the easy student/teacher interaction of Google Apps with G Suite that empowers student creativity and critical thinking. Keeler and Herrington demonstrate fifty ways to bring math classes into the twenty-first century with easy-to-use technology.

Table Talk Math

A Practical Guide for Bringing Math into Everyday Conversations

By John Stevens (@Jstevens009)

In *Table Talk Math*, John Stevens offers parents—and teachers—ideas for initiating authentic, math-based, everyday conversations that get kids to notice and pique their curiosity about the numbers, patterns, and equations in the world around them.

Shift This!

How to Implement Gradual Change for Massive Impact in Your Classroom

By Joy Kirr (@JoyKirr)

Establishing a student-led culture focused on individual responsibility and personalized learning *is* possible, sustainable, and even easy when it happens little by little. In *Shift This!*, Joy Kirr details gradual shifts in thinking, teaching, and approach for massive impact in your classroom.

Unmapped Potential

An Educator's Guide to Lasting Change

By Julie Hasson and Missy Lennard (@PPrincipals)

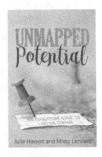

Overwhelmed and overworked? You're not alone, but it can get better. You simply need the right map to guide you from frustrated to fulfilled. *Unmapped Potential* offers advice and practical strategies to forge a unique path to becoming the educator and *person* you want to be.

Shattering the Perfect Teacher Myth

6 Truths That Will Help You THRIVE as an Educator

By Aaron Hogan (@aaron_hogan)

Author and educator Aaron Hogan helps shatter the idyllic "perfect teacher" myth, which erodes self-confidence with unrealistic expectations and sets teachers up for failure. His book equips educators with strategies that help them shift out of survival mode and THRIVE.

Social LEADia

Moving Students from Digital Citizenship to Digital Leadership

By Jennifer Casa-Todd (@JCasaTodd)

A networked society requires students to leverage social media to connect to people, passions, and opportunities to grow and make a difference. *Social LEADia* helps shift focus at school and home from digital citizenship to digital leadership and equip students for the future.

Spark Learning

3 Keys to Embracing the Power of Student Curiosity

By Ramsey Musallam (@ramusallam)

Inspired by his popular TED Talk "3 Rules to Spark Learning," Musallam combines brain science research, proven teaching methods, and his personal story to empower you to improve your students' learning experiences by inspiring inquiry and harnessing its benefits.

Ditch That Homework

Practical Strategies to Help Make Homework Obsolete

By Matt Miller and Alice Keeler (@jmattmiller, @alicekeeler)

In *Ditch That Homework*, Miller and Keeler discuss the pros and cons of homework, why it's assigned, and what life could look like without it. They evaluate research, share parent and teacher insights, then make a convincing case for ditching it for effective and personalized learning methods.

The Four O'Clock Faculty

A Rogue Guide to Revolutionizing Professional Development

By Rich Czyz (@RACzyz)

In *The Four O'Clock Faculty*, Rich identifies ways to make professional learning meaningful, efficient, and, above all, personally relevant. It's a practical guide to revolutionize PD, revealing why some is so awful and what *you* can do to change the model for the betterment of everyone.

Culturize

Every Student. Every Day. Whatever It Takes.

By Jimmy Casas (@casas_jimmy)

Culturize dives into what it takes to cultivate a community of learners who embody innately human traits our world desperately needs—kindness, honesty, and compassion. Casas's stories reveal how "soft skills" can be honed while exceeding academic standards of twenty-first-century learning.

Code Breaker

Increase Creativity, Remix Assessment, and Develop a Class of Coder Ninjas!

By Brian Aspinall (@mraspinall)

You don't have to be a "computer geek" to use coding to turn curriculum expectations into student skills. Use *Code Breaker* to teach students how to identify problems, develop solutions, and use computational thinking to apply and demonstrate learning.

The Wild Card

7 Steps to an Educator's Creative Breakthrough

By Hope and Wade King (@hopekingteach, @wadeking7)

The Kings facilitate a creative breakthrough in the classroom with *The Wild Card*, a step-by-step guide to drawing on your authentic self to deliver your content creatively and be the *wild card* who changes the game for your learners.

Stories from Webb

The Ideas, Passions, and Convictions of a Principal and His School Family

By Todd Nesloney (@TechNinjaTodd)

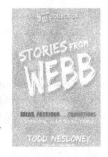

Stories from Webb goes right to the heart of education. Told by award-winning principal Todd Nesloney and his dedicated team of staff and teachers, this book reminds you why you became an educator. Relatable stories reinvigorate and may inspire you to tell your own!

The Principled Principal

10 Principles for Leading Exceptional Schools

By Jeffrey Zoul and Anthony McConnell
(@Jeff_Zoul, @mcconnellaw)

Zoul and McConnell know from personal experience that the role of a school principal is one of the most challenging *and* the most rewarding in education. Using relatable stories and real-life examples, they reveal ten core values that will empower you to work and lead with excellence.

The Limitless School

Creative Ways to Solve the Culture Puzzle

By Abe Hege and Adam Dovico (@abehege, @adamdovico)

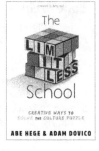

Being intentional about creating a positive culture is imperative for your school's success. This book identifies the nine pillars that support a positive school culture and explains how each stakeholder has a vital role to play in the work of making schools safe, inviting, and dynamic.

Google Apps for Littles

Believe They Can

By Christine Pinto and Alice Keeler
(@PintoBeanz11, @alicekeeler)

Learn how to tap into students' natural curiosity using technology. Pinto and Keeler share a wealth of innovative ways to integrate digital tools in the primary classroom to make learning engaging and relevant for even the youngest of today's twenty-first-century learners.

Be the One for Kids

You Have the Power to Change the Life of a Child

By Ryan Sheehy (@sheehyrw)

Students need guidance to succeed academically, but they also need our help to survive and thrive in today's turbulent world. They need someone to model the attributes that will help them win not just in school but in life as well. That someone is you.

Let Them Speak

How Student Voice Can Transform Your School

By Rebecca Coda and Rick Jetter
(@RebeccaCoda, @RickJetter)

We say, "Student voice matters," but are we really listening? This book will inspire you to find out what your students really think, feel, and need. You'll learn how to listen to and use student feedback to improve your school's culture. All you have to do is ask—and then *Let Them Speak*.

The EduProtocol Field Guide

16 Student-Centered Lesson Frames for Infinite Learning Possibilities

By Marlena Hebren and Jon Corippo

Are you ready to break out of the lesson-and-worksheet rut? Use *The EduProtocol Field Guide* to create engaging and effective instruction, build culture, and deliver content to K–12 students in a supportive, creative environment.

All 4s and 5s

A Guide to Teaching and Leading Advanced Placement Programs

By Andrew Sharos

AP classes shouldn't be relegated to "privileged" schools and students. With proper support, every student can experience success. *All 4s and 5s* offers a wealth of classroom and program strategies that equip you to develop a culture of academic and personal excellence.

Shake Up Learning

Practical Ideas to Move Learning from Static to Dynamic

By Kasey Bell (@ShakeUpLearning)

Is the learning in your classroom static or dynamic? *Shake Up Learning* guides you through the process of creating dynamic learning opportunities—from purposeful planning and maximizing technology to fearless implementation.

The Secret Solution

How One Principal Discovered the Path to Success

Todd Whitaker, Sam Miller, and Ryan Donlan (@ToddWhitaker, @SamMiller29, @RyanDonlan)

An entertaining look at the path to leadership excellence, this parable provides leaders with a non-threatening tool to discuss problematic attitudes in schools. This updated edition includes a reader's guide to help you identify habits and traits that can help you and your team succeed.

The Path to Serendipity

Discover the Gifts along Life's Journey

By Allyson Apsey (@AllysonApsey)

In this funny, genuine, and clever book, Allyson Apsey shares relatable stories and practical strategies for living a meaningful life regardless of the craziness happening around you. You'll discover that you really do have the power to choose the kind of life you live—every day.

The Pepper Effect

Tap into the Magic of Creativity, Collaboration, and Innovation

By Sean Gaillard (@smgaillard)

Using *Sgt. Pepper's Lonely Hearts Club Band* by The Beatles as a template for inspiration, Sean Gaillard explores the necessary steps for creating the conditions for motivation, collaboration, creativity, and innovation in your schoolhouse.

About the Author

Jennifer Burdis is a twenty-year veteran elementary teacher in the San Diego area, a former Penn State Volleyball player, and an athlete who competed in seasons six and seven of *American Ninja Warrior*. As an author and keynote speaker, Jen passionately shares her grit and growth mindset strategies by turning obstacles into opportunities, incorporating more kinesthetic based learning activities, and practicing daily healthy habits as a strong foundation to learning.

As a child with undiagnosed dyslexia, Jen didn't learn how to read until she was working on her master's degree in reading and writing curriculum. Because of her own school experience, Jen understands how students feel when their learning needs aren't being met. She seeks to address the needs of the whole child to ensure students are healthy, safe, engaged, supported, and challenged. She believes that, together, teachers and families can provide students valuable lifelong health and wellness skills that empower them to take charge of their learning.

Jen launched the EduNinja™ 30-Day Health and Wellness Challenge in 2015 to promote healthy habits and fitness activities for teachers, students, and families. Through this challenge, thousands of students, their families, and teachers have learned to live stronger, healthier lives through nutrition, movement, and mindfulness. Learn more about Jen Burdis or sign up for the free EduNinja™ 30-Day Health and Wellness Challenge at eduninja.net.

Connect with Jen:

 eduninja.net

 ninjajenburdis@gmail.com

CPSIA information can be obtained
at www.ICGtesting.com
Printed in the USA
FSHW01n2244060618
49043FS